CHINESE COOKING

FRANK OLIVER

Chinese Cooking

ANDRE DEUTSCH

FIRST PUBLISHED OCTOBER 1955 BY
ANDRE DEUTSCH LIMITED
105 GREAT RUSSELL STREET
LONDON WCI
SECOND IMPRESSION MARCH 1957
THIRD IMPRESSION AUGUST 1959
FOURTH IMPRESSION SEPTEMBER 1960
FIFTH IMPRESSION FEBRUARY 1969
SIXTH IMPRESSION DECEMBER 1971
SEVENTH IMPRESSION AUGUST 1976
COPYRIGHT © 1955 BY FRANK OLIVER
ALL RIGHTS RESERVED
PRINTED PHOTOLITHO IN GREAT BRITAIN BY
EBENEZER BAYLIS AND SON LTD
THE TRINITY PRESS
WORCESTER AND LONDON

ISBN 0 233 95528 3

CONTENTS

CONTENTS

INTRODUCTION

The long-standing argument as to whether Chinese or French gastronomy is the greater is never likely to be settled; less likely now because one can no longer go to China to test the art of the Chinese chef on his home ground, where the chef should always be tested. But the matter of precedence is unimportant. Let us recognize that the Chinese have a superb cuisine and let us enjoy it, no matter in what part of the world we happen to be. I recently went as near China as Hongkong to see what was being done at the country's backdoor, but I found with regret that the Chinese cooking there wasn't what one enjoyed in Peking before the war. But it was good.

What makes Chinese cooking so good is what makes French cooking good; it is full of flavour, something apt to be forgotten by cooks in other places. Chinese cooking does not sacrifice flavour for appearance, a sin in some places. There is also, about Chinese cooking, the same simplicity that one finds in the best French cooking. It is a simplicity achieved by taking infinite pains. Few good dishes are so simple in their final state as Chicken Velvet in China or *blanquette de veau* in France but it is a simplicity achieved at the cost of much work, a lot of time and infinite care. Simplicity, in other words, does not mean something 'whipped up' in ten minutes.

Another similarity between the two schools of cooking is that in neither country do cooks expect to get a first-class dinner out of second-class ingredients. As others have said before me, you cannot get out of a dish more than you put into it. Therefore the cook's job begins not in the kitchen but at the market. The Chinese, again like the French, don't try to take short cuts in their cooking. They don't try to get superb dinners out of highly mechanized kitchens from 'quick frozen'

7

or 'processed' or 'pre-cooked' or 'homogenized' materials. In this century of invention nothing has yet been invented that can take the place of a diligent cook and the Chinese are diligent cooks.

It has been said more than once that some of the finest dishes ever invented originated in countries with low standards of living and that rich countries have made but small contributions to the art of good cooking. This is perhaps largely true but, I think, doesn't go all the way. Two countries with low standards of living that I have visited, Japan and Mongolia, enjoy cooking that must be classed with the worst in the world. My own feeling is that good cooking and culture have a good deal to do with each other. The two things seem to go together naturally. China, heaven knows, has a low standard of living— but it has an old and great culture and even its coolies used to eat palatable food, while that of the average worker was mouth-watering. Many a time I have been in a small Chinese shop and found the proprietor and his assistants round a table at the morning meal and the sight of the food has made me forget what I went in for and my only wish was to sit down with them. Similarly in France it is easy to eat very well in a village or unambitious countryside café.

And why not? Cooking may be a minor art but it is an art and cultured people have an interest in all the arts. The majority of people eat over a thousand meals a year and if a man lives a normal span he has some fifty sentient years in which to enjoy more than 50,000 meals. This surely is a matter of some importance and worthy of considerable time and thought. And the present is as good a time as any for the expenditure of that time and thought. These are servantless days in most parts of the world and more and more people, of both sexes, are doing their own cooking. The advantage is that no longer are they restricted to the national dishes of whatever nation the kitchen factotum came from. They can, working for themselves, range all over the world *via* cookbooks and eat better and more variously than they ever did before.

It is true that cooking is something that does not export perfectly. Abroad it is always approximate and limited but it can still be good. The vegetables may not always be quite the same, some domestic herbs may not be available, but that doesn't mean that the dishes of one country should not be imitated in another; they can and should be tried by the gastronomic adventurer. You cannot possibly achieve in your own kitchen all or half of what is achieved by a cook or body of cooks in a first-class Peking restaurant, but you can achieve a number of things those cooks produced. Not even Chinese cooks seem able to do their best outside their own country. I have been eating oriental cooking for some thirty years and within the past year have eaten meals prepared by Chinese cooks in Honolulu, Hongkong, Singapore, Macassar, San Francisco, New York, Washington and London; but no meal in those cities has come anywhere near equalling the food I got to know in Peking in the 'twenties and 'thirties. The cooking in that period was incomparable. What the attitude of the Chinese communist leaders is towards food I have no means of knowing, but I have a feeling they take more than a passing interest and I suspect that, while they may be for the proletariat in many things, they cheerfully eat better than the coolie. If that is a correct assumption then we may expect, when China once again opens herself to the rest of the world, to find as good cooking as ever in Peking and gastronomic delights will welcome the first visitors to that city in the post-communist phase of its long history.

Even then many of us may not be able to travel so far to get Peking Duck or Chicken Velvet. But we will be able then, as now, to enjoy in our own homes dozens of Chinese dishes that are first-class and for which the ingredients lie ready to hand. The results in our own kitchens won't be as good as they used to be in the best restaurants in China but they will be very good indeed and they can be—I say it with conviction—better than the bulk of food served in many Chinese restaurants in the western world.

One thing to be remembered about Chinese cooking is that it is never intended to produce one main dish for stuffing the diner. The Chinese never goes in for the Chinese equivalent of a steak 'that thick' (finger and thumb two inches apart). He wants a few mouthfuls of each of several dishes. The ordinary evening meal of a Chinese family in modest circumstances may well consist of four or five dishes whereas the equivalent meal of a London or New York family in similar financial circumstances would consist of no more than two dishes. The Londoner or New Yorker visiting a good restaurant for a celebration might have four or five courses. The Chinese, entertaining honoured guests, would provide not less than fifteen dishes and on extra-special occasions even thirty or more.

The largest Chinese banquet I ever attended ran to thirty-four dishes and I tasted twenty-eight of them without overeating. Of some one ate a mouthful, of others four or five. But the whole was a delight, a fascinating journey through Chinese cuisine.

Many people consider Chinese food too exotic to be attempted in the ordinary household kitchen but nothing could be further from the truth. Chinese food can be very exotic, for it covers a wide area, all the way from the ultra-exotic to the extremely plain and simple. It would be easy in this book to give a recipe which begins, 'Take thirty duck tongues . . .' for the purpose of making duck tongue soup. But you will not find it here because there are few if any cooks who expect to be serving thirty ducks from which to reserve thirty tongues. The idea has been to give as wide and varied a range of Chinese dishes as possible which can be made by any good cook from ingredients that can be obtained without difficulty. Some are very plain and simple; others may be termed slightly exotic. But even the exotic ones are not difficult and are well worth trying. Remember that no man's taste in food and wine is better than the education his stomach has received and Chinese cooking is an interesting and tasty course in one's taste education.

The Chinese argue eternally about which regional cooking is best. Cantonese cooking (or Kwangtung cooking, to name the province), is undoubtedly the best-known outside China because the Cantonese are the travellers and emigrants of China. The great bulk of all overseas Chinese come from South China and consequently the great majority of Chinese restaurants in cities like London, New York, Chicago, San Francisco, Hongkong, Singapore and the cities of Malaya and Indonesia, serve only Cantonese food. Any Cantonese will argue for his regional cuisine at any time and in any place. And very good indeed it is, but there is other regional cooking in China that is as good and some of it, in my view at least, is better. If forced to a choice I might argue for Shantung cooking as the best but I'd rather not argue at all and enjoy all of it.

Those foreigners who had the luck to live in Peking in the good years could enjoy any Chinese regional cooking. It was all there, restaurants serving food as cooked in Kwangtung, Fukien, Honan, Kiangsu, Shantung and Szechuen among the more famous. Peking was for Chinese food what Paris is for French food. In Paris you get the cream of all French cooking and Peking restaurants provided the cream of all Chinese cooking. I never had the good fortune to visit Szechuen province but Peking had more than one good Szechuenese restaurant and to them I remain indebted for my first taste of superb dishes from that far-away western province.

It must be true that provincial cooking that transfers itself from province to metropolis changes over a period, especially after a century or two, but I think it loses only some of its characteristics. One must remember too that while it may be slightly different it may also be better, for refinement carried not too far can improve.

And in any event, Chinese cuisine like any other is a constantly changing affair. Up to a very few years ago the Chinese were largely illiterate but they were none the less educated and informed. Their storied history went down from generation to generation and century to century by word of mouth. So did their cooking, from master chef to youthful apprentice (usually a son or nephew of the chef). How far back good cooking goes in China would be hard to determine but the Chinese were early discoverers of fire and they have been farmers for forty centuries. They probably were eating in a civilized and varied way while our rude forefathers in Europe were tearing raw flesh to pieces and eating fruit and nuts off bushes and trees.

Chinese cuisine has changed a good deal even in this century. A number of vegetables regarded now as domestic by the younger generation were unknown to their grand-parents. Chinese cooking has benefited thereby because the field of possibility has been enlarged. At least one good vegetable was exported from China in moderately good form and was later re-imported in much improved form. This is the Shantung cabbage or *pai tsai* (white cabbage). I believe the seed of this vegetable was exported to America many years ago and there widely grown and cultivated until it was much superior to its Chinese ancestor. This improved variety went back to China in the form of seed and for many years now has been a winter standby in North China. In the autumn it is cut in large numbers before the heavy frosts descend, and is stored in pits roofed over with bamboo and straw. Through the icy Peking winters it was possible to enjoy fresh cabbage until the Spring brought new green stuff. As the hard winter wore on some of the outside leaves rotted but the inside was always as fresh and crisp and ivory white as it was the day it was cut. It is an incomparable cabbage.

To many elderly Chinese celery, tomatoes and cucumbers are still new and foreign vegetables but the younger Chinese regard them as native.

The recipes herein come from all parts of China and no effort has been made to indicate the places where they originated. Indeed in some instances it would not be possible to say where they came from originally. In a number of instances substitutes for original Chinese ingredients have been given. This doesn't mean it isn't Chinese food. Use what ingredients you have but cook them in the Chinese way with Chinese seasonings, sauces and garnishes and the result will have the authentic Chinese flavour. And nowadays so many Chinese cooking ingredients are available in tins or in dried form. They can't compare with the fresh but they still are very good.

A great lack in Chinese cooking outside China is the absence of Chinese yellow rice wine, known either as *Huang Chiu* or *Shao Hsing*. In its native habitat it is an excellent *vin du pays* when well matured, and is used freely in cooking and as an accompaniment to the finished products of the kitchen. Its fault is that it will not cross the seas and retain its qualities. I have yet to find a good bottle in London or New York. European wines do not go as well with Chinese food but some of them are far far better than no wine at all. Red wines I find do not go at all well but there are some white wines that go very pleasantly with a Chinese dinner. They must not be too sweet. So far as my experiments have gone Rhine wines *auslese* are too sweet but *spatlese* I find very good. Of French wines the best with Chinese dishes I find a dry Graves. Chinese yellow rice wine is something like a medium dry sherry, though with a somewhat rougher taste, and it is served warm. You can serve a medium dry sherry all through the meal but I find the white wines recommended above much better. There is sometimes available a Chinese distilled spirit known variously as *pai gar*, *kaoliang* and Tatung spirit. Its alcoholic content is well over 90 per cent, it has a curious and—to me—unpleasant smell and taste, its powers of intoxication are enormous and they operate swiftly. It is of little use in cooking and hardly suitable for drinking with meals. In China my Chinese friends drank it after dinner as a liqueur and fortunate it sometimes was that the usual mode of travel homeward was by ricksha, because that is the handiest vehicle into which to place a well-dined man who suddenly finds that his legs lack bones.

For the Chinese there is one supreme meat, pork. When he

uses the word meat he means pork and nothing else. Those Chinese who can afford it eat it almost every day. It never palls. The poorer Chinese dream about eating pork. That acute observer of things Chinese, Dr A. F. Legendre, writing many years ago from Szechuen said that when 'poor wretched starveling coolies are discussing among themselves the number and quality of the material enjoyments of the Son of Heaven they never fail to cite the extraordinary happiness of being always able to buy every day for his dinner a hundred thousand pounds of fat pork.'

Of the feathered meats the Chinese loves above all others duck and chicken. Beef he eats occasionally, veal almost never, mutton and lamb occasionally (unless he is of the Mohammedan faith when he eats it constantly). Pheasant and partridge find their way into the Chinese kitchen occasionally as do goose and turkey. Venison is eaten occasionally and bustard can always be found in northern markets during the winter. Pigeon is highly regarded and considered something of a luxury. Fish is a favourite food, both fresh and salt water varieties with the former the more popular. The Chinese eats large quantities of vegetables. Buddhist monks are vegetarians for religious reasons but the Chinese is rarely a vegetarian by choice though often by economic necessity. Many Chinese live on vegetables and grain foods the year long but it is usually because they are poor and cannot afford meat or fish. Even those on whom vegetarianism is forced by painful economic facts try to save up a few coins with which to buy a tiny piece of pork with which to celebrate the New Year.

Rice is, of course, an important article of diet for most of the world. The daily use of rice begins at the eastern end of the Mediterranean and continues through the Middle East, India, South-East Asia, Indonesia and Japan. As far as China is concerned not a few Chinese in the south get little else at least six days a week. It is the same story in the Yangtze valley. In North China its use is not quite so frequent. Much rice is eaten there but also some wheat, some barley, a great deal of maize and a great deal of millet, both the small millet and the giant variety whose stalks grow six to eight feet high in North China and up to twelve feet in Manchuria, that garden of Asia. Very little rice is grown in North China and its importation from other parts makes it something of a luxury for the poor.

But generally speaking rice is a basic food. It does not accompany a Chinese meal as bread does a European meal. For the poor and the middle class it is the main dish, helped down by a few vegetables, a trifle of meat or fish and a little soup. In middle class homes there will be a large bowl of it for each member of the family and then in the middle of the table from three to five dishes, communal pots into which all dip with their chopsticks. On the other hand, at banquets rice is never served until the end of the meal, to fill up any cranny that remains—and it is good manners to eat every grain of it.

These Chinese are great domestic economists. They discovered long ago that a given quantity of grain has several times the food value eaten directly and will feed five times as many people as it would if fed to stock and brought to the table in the shape of meat and milk. They therefore eat a great deal of grain and vegetables and much less meat than the meat-eating peoples of Europe and America. Population pressure has always been with them and famine has devastated their economy many times. These things have taught them the best uses of what their land produces and their adventurousness, ingenuity and imagination in the kitchen have developed through the centuries a remarkably good and very various cuisine. Philosophy runs like a thread through all Chinese life and living, including eating; an old Chinese saying has it that those who live on vegetables get strong, those who live on meat become brave, those who live on grain acquire wisdom and those who live on air become divine. If there is good basis for this then the recipes which follow should enable you to be strong, brave and wise and divinity can be left to take care of itself.

FRANK OLIVER

GENERAL HINTS

It is not easy to say, in the following recipes, whether the quantities given are sufficient for two, four or six people because it depends whether you are eating in Chinese or western style. If you are eating in Chinese style it means that you will have not less than eight dishes on the menu. In that event eight dishes made of the quantities given in these recipes will provide an ample dinner for six people.

If, on the other hand, you are cooking for just two people then one soup, one or two main dishes and a small dessert will be plenty. Given these points of departure the hostess can quickly tell how many dishes will be needed for parties of four, eight or ten people.

Perhaps it is well to say that these recipes, like all recipes in all cookbooks, are what may be termed 'general policy rules'. Great chefs never seem to mind giving out their recipes because they realize they are giving but general directions and that no two cooks following the same recipe exactly are likely to produce identical dishes. All good cooks work a great deal by 'sense' and 'feel' no matter what recipes they are using. All good cooks are individualists and their products individual. These recipes are sound general policy rules and result from having cooked and eaten more Chinese meals than can possibly be remembered. They have been collected in such diverse places as Peking, Shanghai, Hongkong, Indonesia, London, San Francisco, New York and Washington D.C.

A noted writer of English once said that grammar follows the language and not language the grammar and one might paraphrase him and say that recipes follow good cooking rather than good cooking following a recipe slavishly. Good cooking is a live art and adventurous, demanding a measure of imagination which cannot make its contribution to good living and good eating if recipes are to be followed with the exactitude of a chemist filling a prescription. The newcomer to Chinese cooking will soon develop his own individual touches but his dishes will still be essentially Chinese because of ingredients and methods of cooking.

Many Chinese recipes call for Chinese wine but generally speaking it can't be obtained in European countries or America and so sherry, the nearest substitute available, is given herein for all recipes calling for *shao shing* or yellow rice wine. But please don't buy what is sometimes known as 'cooking sherry'. If you ask why, I suggest you go to a modest French restaurant and eat their *boeuf à la bourguignonne*. Then eat it in a first class restaurant (or in your own home) made with a Chambertin of a good year. In a rash and gay moment I once made this dish with a Romanée Conti of a moderately good year. Unforgettable. The difference in Chinese food in which so-called cooking sherry is used and that in which good sherry is used is a very great deal more than the difference in price between the two bottles. Some cooks used to European cooking methods may feel that the cooking times given here are very short. They are. Vegetables especially are cooked quickly and with only small amounts of liquid. They come to the table fresh and crisp, complete with vitamins and minerals and, equally important, full flavour and they are easily digestible.

Wherever the word oil is used it refers to peanut oil, most commonly used in China. It is both cheap and a very good cooking medium. Soya bean oil is equally good if not better but it is usually more expensive. Sesame oil can also be used and this is specified in some recipes. These oils are the best for Chinese cooking but if they are not available you can use the tea seed oil sold in England for frying, or even ordinary lard, but get peanut oil if possible. I have never found modern vegetable shortening put up in tins particularly good in cooking Chinese food, and olive oil has rather too strong a flavour for Chinese dishes.

It must be remembered that in Chinese cooking no food is put into oil until the oil is quite hot and also that, unless a recipe calls for simmering slowly under a cover, the food is constantly turned in the pan, but is turned with reasonable care so that the cooking food is not broken up or made mushy in consistency.

By and large the Chinese are much fonder of garlic than any Europeans and quite a good deal goes into their food. Almost invariably they use more than suits a European palate. In the recipes in this book I have reduced the quantities to what seem to me to be general European taste but, of course, the cook can easily increase or decrease the amount given.

Many Chinese recipes call for the addition of a little sugar, for they realize what many Europeans don't, that it helps to bring out flavour as does salt. Almost any Chinese dish is improved by the addition of half a teaspoonful.

Soy sauce is used more than any other single ingredient in Chinese cooking. Large quantities are used in all Chinese kitchens. Not only does it lend a special flavour to the food but it is quite salty. For this reason less salt is used than would be put into European dishes.

The products of the cow are almost unknown in Chinese kitchens. Chinese cooks never use butter, nor milk, nor cream nor cheese though the new generation of Chinese are gradually taking to that almost universal dessert, ice cream. What Europeans get, nutritionally, from milk and milk products the Chinese get from the wonderful soya bean which is eaten as a bean, as bean sprouts, as bean curd and as soy sauce. Visitors to China have often wondered how a Chinese coolie could do such a hard day's work as he did on a diet that contained neither meat nor cheese. The answer is that the soya bean gives him the necessary protein.

In buying soy sauce be sure to get a good quality. Of late years a great deal of synthetic soy sauce has appeared on the markets of the world. Use it if you have to but get the genuine article if possible.

In many Chinese food shops one can buy a flavouring powder called *Ve-Tsin*. Its purpose is not to give a different flavour to the food but to bring out the natural flavours as strongly as possible. A similar powder is marketed in some places under the name of *Mei Yen*. Yet again there is a European and American product called *Accent* which is in the same category. For many years a Japanese powder has been marketed under the name of *Ajinimoto*. The basis of these powders is monosodium glutamate. Any one of these mentioned can be added to Chinese dishes with advantage, except of course, the sweet desserts. It is now so commonly used by Chinese cooks I have not mentioned it in individual recipes but its use is strongly recommended.

Another matter of some importance is ginger. This is used in scores of Chinese dishes and there is really no good substitute for fresh ginger root. Two or three thin slices lend a good deal of enchantment and flavour. There are bound to be times and places when it is not available and when it is missing the cook can decide whether to use a touch of ground ginger or a piece of preserved ginger chopped up. I prefer the latter. If you do use preserved ginger get the kind preserved in syrup. Wash off the syrup and either slice it finely or chop it up.

Fresh bamboo shoot is never likely to be available but the tinned shoots are exceedingly good and are exported from both China and Japan, sometimes whole, sometimes sliced. Use the whole if possible. In their natural state they are like giant asparagus when cut, two to five inches in diameter at the bottom and sometimes almost a foot long. The tinned ones are usually about three inches long and are ready to use, requiring no trimming.

A word or two about kitchen utensils may be useful. In their own kitchens the Chinese do not have modern gas and electric stoves. Millions of them manage and manage very well with primitive stoves that burn briquettes made of coal dust and clay. I don't suggest anything so primitive but I do suggest that gas is easier to use than electricity because of the instan-

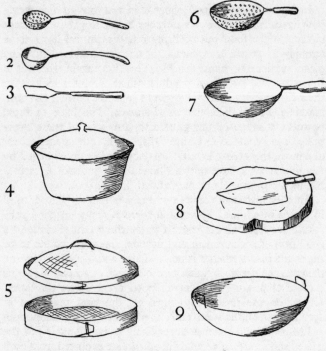

1 Small strainer
2 Chinese kitchen ladle
3 Spatula for turning frying food
4 Chinese earthenware saucepan
5 Wooden steamer
6 Large strainer
7 Chinese frying pan
8 Chopping block
9 Cast iron saucepan

taneous control of the flame. The Chinese use cast iron cooking pots and it is my experience that this type is much better than modern ones of aluminium and other new metals. The usual ones are deep and concave with a wooden handle and seldom flat-bottomed like ours; but as concave ones are not likely to be found readily I would suggest that wherever possible the oldfashioned iron frying pans and iron saucepans be used. These old pans or skillets seldom had covers but a tin or enamel saucepan lid the same size as the pan does perfectly well.

The best tool for turning food in the pan is a small flat shovel affair, rather like a small pancake turner, the blade about three inches square.

When a recipe calls for steaming this does not mean a double boiler. It means the old-fashioned affair with the bottom of the top saucepan perforated so that the steam circulates round the food being steamed, or else a rack which suspends the steaming food above the water in the pan.

The Chinese, when it comes to kitchen tools, use even heavier knives than you find in French kitchens, large, sharp, and weighty. They believe in letting the weight of the tool do the work rather than using muscular force with a small light knife. They pass root vegetables at great speed under a heavy knife and the sheer weight of the blade cuts through it cleanly and quickly. There is never any sawing back and forth across the board or chopping block. Sharp *heavy* knives were the first labour saving tools.

For reasons I can't quite explain it always seems better to eat Chinese food in the Chinese way. Chinese table dishes are better designed than anything else for serving Chinese food and in any city where there is a sizeable Chinese community you are sure to find a shop selling such dishes. The deep dishes in which soups are served have straight sides like some French casseroles used for soufflés and the dishes in which other foods are served are usually oval in shape and stand on a short pedestal.

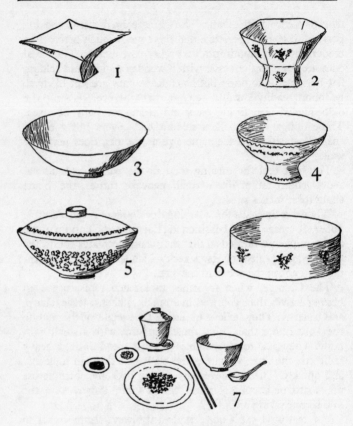

1, 2, 3 and 4: Chinese serving dishes
5 and 6: Chinese dishes for serving soups
7: A place setting at a Chinese table

Bowls for rice are rather like large Chinese teacups. Each diner requires a rice bowl, a Chinese teacup, a small plate and a pair of chopsticks. For soups the Chinese use a porcelain spoon. They are cheap and very useful in a dozen ways. In addition a table needs at least four very small dishes about the size of the saucer belonging to a small coffee cup. In these put fresh mustard and that mixture of pepper and salt into which food is dipped from the chopsticks on its way from dish to mouth.

Chinese dining tables are usually round. These are both better for general conversation and also they place each diner the same distance from the food dishes which are placed in the centre. Host and hostess sit together and face the guests of honour across the table. Host and hostess usually have an extra pair of chopsticks apiece with which to pass special delicacies to guests. When soup is served an extra rice bowl is given to each diner.

Chopsticks, westerners in China used to say, made Chinese food taste better than when eaten with fork and spoon. I can't say them nay. The best chopsticks are still the cheapest—plain bamboo, the top half squared, the other half rounded. Almost all Chinese food is cut into small pieces for quick cooking and for ease in eating with chopsticks. It isn't difficult to learn to use them and they are exceedingly useful tools in the kitchen. Lay the bottom chopstick from the tip of the second finger to the second joint of the thumb. This one is held firmly and does not move. Now place the upper chopstick between the tip of the forefinger and the tip of the thumb. The first joint of the forefinger presses the tip of the top chopstick down on the tip of the bottom one to grip the food between the points. Hold them lightly but firmly and don't strain the muscles or you'll have something like tennis elbow in the hand. It may seem a trifle awkward at first but soon becomes easy and handier than using fork or spoon. In the kitchen Chinese cooks use them for beating eggs and they invariably keep a metal pair for adding small coals to the kitchen fire.

1 Chinese rice or soup bowl
2 Chinese porcelain soup spoon
3 Chinese condiment dish
4 Chinese teacup with cover

Menus have been suggested that are good for lunch or dinner. No breakfast menus are given because I doubt if any Europeans would care much for Chinese breakfasts. They consist usually of rice gruel or congee and a few salty and savoury things. In many places Chinese eat no breakfast beyond morning tea. They eat twice a day, mid-morning and late afternoon.

If any reader searches herein for chop suey dishes he or she is going to be disappointed. As far as I have been able to gather chop suey is an American invention and I've never met a Chinese who didn't disown it and turn up his nose at it. I never heard the term used in China and never saw it written until I landed in San Francisco some years ago. I have eaten it and can't remember it ever being the least bit interesting. Chinese restaurants seem to serve it because they think it is what foreigners want or because it is what many foreigners believe Chinese food to be. Its birthplace is said to be San Francisco, which is small credit to that fair and pleasant city.

In cutting many vegetables the Chinese employ what is known as the 'rolling' cut. Use a heavy knife at an angle and cut an inch off (for instance) a carrot, then roll the carrot half-way over and make the second cut, roll again and make a third and so on. This gives more interesting shapes and the sliced pieces will not stick together as they usually do when sliced plainly squarely across the vegetable.

A very large selection of Chinese foodstuffs, including noodles, bean curd, green ginger, various kinds of dried fish and mushrooms, sauces, spices, even dried squid, tinned abalone and Chinese preserved eggs are now available in London. Shops where they may be obtained are:

The Hong Kong Emporium
53 Rupert Street, London W1
(who also sell Chinese table ware, chopsticks etc.)

Orientalia
22 Rupert Street, London W1

The Little Pulteney Stores
27 Brewer Street, London W1

A. Gomez Ortega
74-76 Old Compton Street, London W1

Stocks vary a good deal in these stores, and something not available in one shop will probably be found in the next. The food departments of Harrods and Selfridges also have a selection of Chinese tinned foods.

In the lists of ingredients for these recipes, 'a cup' is eight fluid ounces.

HORS D'OEUVRE

Most Chinese hors d'oeuvre are cold dishes. At banquets as many as twenty-four may be produced but at ordinary dinners the number is usually four, placed in the centre of the round dining-table for guests to pick at with chopsticks while the cooks put the finishing touches to the dinner.

In addition to a selection of those dishes mentioned below serve also small dishes of melon seeds if available and such things as apricot almonds if available, or pine nuts, or salted peanuts. Pickled vegetables are also often put on among cold hors d'oeuvre, but the sour variety, not the sweet.

SLICED HAM

½ *lb. sliced ham*   1 *teaspoon sesame oil*
½ *teaspoon soy sauce*

The ham should be of the Smithfield or York type, well cured, and can be cooked or uncooked. Slice very thinly in small pieces. Place the pieces on a small dish and pour over them the mixed oil and soy sauce.

COLD CHICKEN

4 *ozs. cooked chicken, white*   1 *tablespoon soy sauce*
  meat   1 *teaspoon sesame oil*

Cut thinly small slices of the chicken, place on a serving dish and pour the mixed oil and soy sauce over.

CELERY

1 *head of celery*
1 *teaspoon sesame oil*

1 *tablespoon soy sauce*
½ *teaspoon salt*

Discard the outer leaves of celery and cut the inside stalks into pieces an inch and a half long, splitting them down the middle if they are large. Scald them in boiling water for one minute and then chill them. Place them on a serving dish and then pour mixture of oil, soy sauce and salt over them.

CELERY AND SHRIMP

1 *head celery*
2 *tablespoons soy sauce*
½ *teaspoon sesame oil*

2 *tablespoons chopped cooked shrimp*
1 *teaspoon vinegar*

Wash the celery and cut the tender stalks into sections an inch and a half long. Mix the other ingredients and pour over the celery.

PRESERVED EGGS

4 *preserved eggs*
2 *tablespoons vinegar*

1 *tablespoon chopped ginger*

These eggs, known as *p'i tan*, can often be bought in Chinese food shops. Remove the shell and cut each egg into six pieces, lengthwise, so they resemble sections of an orange. Arrange them on a dish, mix the other ingredients and pour over the eggs.

These are commonly known as 'thousand year eggs' but in fact they are usually thirty or forty days old. The whites are grey but translucent.

BEAN CURD AND SHRIMP

1 *small tin bean curd*
2 *tablespoons soy sauce*
1 *teaspoon sesame oil*

2 *tablespoons finely chopped*
   shrimp

Cut the bean curd into slices and place in a sieve so that it can easily be dipped into boiling water for about two seconds. Chill it and arrange on a serving dish. Mix the other ingredients together and pour over the bean curd.

CANTONESE SAUSAGE

½ *lb. Cantonese sausage*

This can often be bought in Cantonese food shops. Wash the sausage and steam it for 15 minutes. Then chill it and slice thinly, diagonally so that the slices are oval. Serve cold.

COLD DUCK

1 *medium duck*
¼ *cup soy sauce*
2 *tablespoons sherry*
salt to taste

3 *cups water*
1 *teaspoon sugar*
1 *small onion*

Wash the duck and put in a pot with the water. Bring to the boil and add all other ingredients except the sugar. Simmer for an hour and then add the sugar. Simmer for another 45 minutes and then leave the duck to cool in the sauce. Remove the duck and when it is thoroughly cold slice the breast across the grain in slices about half an inch wide. Arrange these on a serving dish as if the breast were whole and serve.

MARINATED SALMON

1 *lb. fresh salmon*
2 *tablespoons soy sauce*
½ *teaspoon finely chopped*
  ginger
1 *tablespoon sesame oil*

1 *spring onion*
2 *tablespoons sherry*
½ *teaspoon salt*
pepper to taste

With a very sharp knife cut the salmon very thinly as you would smoked salmon. Mix all the other ingredients together, chopping the spring onion finely. Lay the salmon slices in it and leave them to marinate for at least fifteen minutes. Remove and serve.

¶ CHICKEN

CHESTNUT CHICKEN

1 *medium chicken*	1 *tablespoon chopped ginger*
4 *mushrooms*	4 *tablespoons soy sauce*
20 *chestnuts*	1 *teaspoon salt*
2 *tablespoons oil*	1 *tablespoon cornflour*
1 *teaspoon sugar*	3 *cups cold water*
1 *onion sliced*	

Clean the chicken, remove the legs and separate them at the joint. With a cleaver cut the chicken in half from the back and then cut each half into three pieces, complete with bone.

Heat a frying pan and add the oil. When hot, sauté the onion until light brown. Then add the chicken pieces and mushrooms and fry for five minutes. Add the salt, sugar, sherry, soy sauce, chestnuts and the cornflour mixed in a little water. Fry until the chicken browns. Lastly add the water and simmer the dish until the chicken is tender.

When the chicken is done there should be about a cup of sauce remaining. Arrange the chicken and chestnuts on a dish, pour the sauce over and serve immediately.

B

CHICKEN VELVET

1 *good sized chicken*
1 *teaspoon cornflour*
water
SAUCE:
1 *cup rich chicken broth*
1 *teaspoon sherry*

10 *egg whites*
½ *cup oil*
1 *teaspoon salt*

½ *teaspoon salt*
1 *tablespoon cornflour*

Remove the breast from the chicken and put the rest of the bird in a saucepan with three cups of water and simmer until a rich stock is made.

Put the breast meat into a mortar and beat with a pestle—or use a heavy wooden bowl and beat it with a hammer or cleaver. Beat at least fifteen minutes, removing any tendons that show. If the meat tends to become dry add water a drop at a time. When this process is complete the meat should be of such a consistency that it will blend easily with the dry cornflour, salt and two unbeaten egg whites. Mix these ingredients with a fork, very slowly adding a half cup of water in the same way that oil is added in making mayonnaise. If it is added too quickly the mixture will not hold together. If you prefer mixing with a wire whisk that is even better than using a fork.

Then beat the remaining eight egg whites until they are quite stiff and add them to the chicken mixture, blending well.

Heat an iron frying pan and add the oil. When it is warm but before it gets very hot put in the egg and chicken mixture. Remove the pan almost immediately and beat the mixture rapidly so that it absorbs the oil thoroughly. Return to the fire and cook over a moderate flame for ten seconds, no longer. Put the chicken mixture into a sieve so that any excess oil drains away. Reheat the pan and add the chicken stock and 1 tablespoon of oil. Stir constantly until it boils and then add the chicken mixture. When this is heated through serve immediately, covering it with the sauce blended in the frying pan.

CHICKEN IN PAPER I

breast of 1 *large chicken*
1 *tablespoon soy sauce*
½ *cup oil*
1 *tablespoon sherry*

pine nuts
*several four-inch squares of
  greaseproof paper*

Cut the chicken meat into pieces about an inch square and an eighth of an inch thick and soak for a few minutes in a mixture of the sherry and soy sauce. Put a pine nut in each piece of meat and then put it diagonally on a square of paper and wrap it up like a *billet doux*. Heat the oil in a frying pan and fry the packages for two or three minutes. Serve in the paper packet, which can easily be opened with chopsticks.

CHICKEN IN PAPER II

Proceed exactly as above but in the mixture for soaking the chicken put a chopped spring onion and some chopped ginger. Leave out the pine nut but in the packet with the chicken put a tiny piece of the chopped ginger.

FRIED SLICED CHICKEN

breast of 1 chicken
1 bamboo shoot
6 water chestnuts
3 tablespoons soy sauce
1 tablespoon sherry
1 lb. of fat pork

6 mushrooms
3 eggs
2 teaspoons cornflour
2 cups oil
salt to taste

Chop the bamboo shoot, water chestnuts and mushrooms and place in a bowl. Add the soy sauce, cornflour, sherry, the egg whites and the salt.

Slice thinly the chicken breast and the pork. On each strip of pork put a teaspoon of the vegetable mixture, which should be stirred well. Then over the teaspoon of mixture place a slice of chicken. Beat the egg yolks and dip each piece of pork, vegetable and chicken in it and fry in deep fat until brown.

PINEAPPLE CHICKEN

1 *medium sized chicken*
2 *small onions*
4 *tablespoons pineapple juice*
MIX TOGETHER:
2 *teaspoons cold water*
1 *teaspoon cornflour*
1 *teaspoon salt*

12 *water chestnuts*
4 *slices tinned pineapple*
1 *stalk celery*

2 *teaspoons soy sauce*
oil

Remove all meat, white and dark, from the chicken and cut it into small diagonal pieces. Smear with the mixture of cornflour, salt and soy sauce. Put 1 tablespoon oil in a hot pan and fry the onion for one minute and then remove. Fry the celery cut in half inch pieces and the sliced water chestnuts for one minute and remove. Then fry the chicken in 2 tablespoons of oil for two minutes and return the vegetables to the pan. Lastly add the pineapple, cutting each slice into six pieces, and the juice, and fry until the pineapple is heated through.

Throughout the cooking process keep the ingredients in the frying pan turning over so they do not burn and be sure the vegetables don't get too well done. Serve hot.

CHICKEN WITH BAMBOO SHOOT

breast of 1 *large chicken*
¼ *lb. mushrooms*
1 *tablespoon sherry*
1 *teaspoon salt*
3 *tablespoons oil*
3 *slices fresh ginger*

small can bamboo shoots
1 *tablespoon cornflour*
2 *tablespoons water*
2 *tablespoons soy sauce*
1 *spring onion*

Cut the chicken breast into thin slices and mix it gently with mixture of cornflour, sherry, water, salt, chopped onion and ginger. Put 1 tablespoon oil into a hot frying pan and add mushrooms (sliced) and the soy sauce. Cook for two minutes, stirring constantly, and then remove. Put 2 tablespoons oil into the pan and when quite hot put in the chicken and cook for one minute, constantly stirring. Then add the bamboo shoots, sliced, and cook for one minute more. Add the mushrooms to the pan and cook for a few seconds longer. Serve immediately.

CHICKEN WITH MUSHROOMS

Proceed exactly as above but leave out the bamboo shoots and increase the quantity of mushrooms to half a pound.

FRIED CHICKEN

2 *young chickens*
2 *tablespoons soy sauce*
1 *medium onion*
½ *teaspoon sugar*

3 *tablespoons sherry*
1 *cup flour*
1 *teaspoon salt*
1 *cup oil*

With a heavy cleaver cut chickens into halves and then into pieces about two inches square, cutting right through the bone. Put pieces into a bowl and sprinkle with chopped onion, sherry, soy sauce, salt and sugar. Stand in a cool place for at least an hour. Then dip each piece of chicken into the flour until it is nicely covered, drop into hot deep fat and fry for two minutes. Serve hot.

CHICKEN WITH GINGER

1 *medium chicken*
2 *cups water*
5 *tablespoons soy sauce*
3 *medium sized pieces ginger*

2 *tablespoons oil*
1 *tablespoon sugar*
2 *tablespoons sherry*
1 *small onion*

Cut the chicken up as in the previous recipe. Heat the oil in a heavy pan and add the chicken. Cook for five minutes, stirring constantly. Then add the ginger slices, the water, soy sauce, sherry and chopped onion. Turn the flame low and cover tightly and let cook for 20 minutes. Finally add the sugar and cook for another ten minutes, or longer if chicken is not then tender.

STEWED CHICKEN

legs and wings of 1 chicken
3 tablespoons soy sauce
2 tablespoons oil
1 clove garlic, chopped
2 medium potatoes, cubed

1 tablespoon sugar
2 cups water
1 onion, sliced
1 tablespoon chopped ginger

With a cleaver cut the chicken into two-inch pieces, bones and all. Add the oil to a hot frying pan and cook the onion, garlic and ginger until lightly brown. Add the chicken pieces and sauté for 1 minute. Then add sugar and water and simmer for 20 minutes. Add the cubed potatoes and serve as soon as the potatoes are cooked.

CHICKEN WITH ALMONDS

breast of 1 chicken
1 sweet green pepper
1 white turnip
½ cup blanched almonds
¼ cup oil
SAUCE:
½ cup chicken stock
1 tablespoon soy sauce
1 tablespoon sherry

10 water chestnuts
1 medium bamboo shoot
1 onion
1 teaspoon salt

2 teaspoons cornflour
½ teaspoon sugar

Heat a heavy frying pan, add a little oil and fry the blanched almonds until they are a light brown. Remove, drain and reserve. Cut the green pepper into pieces about three quarters of an inch square, cube the turnip and cut the water chestnuts into quarters. Slice the onion and cut the chicken into half inch cubes or a little larger.

Heat the frying pan again, add 2 tablespoons of oil and fry the onion until light brown. Add the chicken and fry until the edges begin to brown, then add 2 tablespoons of oil and the vegetables. Cook gently, stirring constantly, for 5 or 6 minutes. Blend the sauce ingredients together and add to the pan together with the almonds. Continue to simmer gently, still stirring, until the sauce thickens. Serve immediately.

WALNUT CHICKEN

1 *medium chicken*
4 *tablespoons chicken stock*
2 *tablespoons sherry*
½ *teaspoon salt*
⅓ *cup sliced mushrooms*
½ *cup chopped celery*
6 *water chestnuts*

1 *cup shelled walnuts*
3 *tablespoons soy sauce*
1 *tablespoon cornflour*
1 *cup oil*
½ *cup sliced bamboo shoots*
1 *medium onion*

Clean the chicken and remove all meat from the bones. Cut the meat into half-inch cubes. Make a mixture of the soy sauce, salt, sherry and cornflour and soak the cubed meat in it for a minute or two. Blanch the walnuts and fry in deep fat which is very hot so they brown quickly. Then drain them.

Into the hot frying pan put 2 tablespoons of oil and then add all the vegetables, cubed or sliced. Fry them until they are about half done and remove. Return the pan to the fire and add 2 tablespoons oil and fry the chicken over a moderate flame until it is cooked. Then add to the pan the stock, vegetables and walnuts. Heat through and serve immediately.

CHICKEN CURRY

1 *medium chicken*
2 *tablespoons oil*
2 *tablespoons sugar*
4 *tablespoons shredded coconut*
2 *tablespoons soy sauce*
¼ *teaspoon salt*

2 *onions*
1 *green onion top*
3 *tablespoons curry powder*
¼ *cup evaporated milk*
1 *bay leaf*
2 *cups water*

Wash the chicken well, remove the legs and separate at the joint. Cut the chicken in half and then each half into four pieces complete with bone. Heat a frying pan and add the oil. When hot add the onion, sliced, and the onion top cut into inch lengths. Then add the chicken and cook for 1 minute. Add the soy sauce, sugar, curry powder and salt and fry for a few seconds more. Then add the bay leaf, the milk and the water. Cover, turn down the flame and cook slowly until the chicken is tender. Serve immediately.

LYCHEE OR LI CHIH CHICKEN

1 *medium chicken*	1 *onion*
12 *water chestnuts*	2 *tablespoons cornflour*
2 *tablespoons soy sauce*	2 *egg whites*
2 *teaspoons sherry*	1 *tin lychees*
1 *cup oil*	½ *teaspoon salt*

SAUCE:

½ *cup syrup from lychees*	1 *tablespoon soy sauce*
¼ *cup chicken stock*	2 *teaspoons cornflour*

Take all meat from the chicken and chop it finely or if you prefer put it through a mincer coarsely. Chop finely the water chestnuts and the onion and add to the chicken with the salt, soy sauce, cornflour, sherry and egg whites. Mix thoroughly and then form into balls.

Heat a frying pan, add oil fairly deep and when it is hot fry the chicken balls (the oil should just cover) until they are golden brown and then remove and drain. Arrange them on a warm serving dish and garnish with the lychees.

Reheat the pan and add 1 tablespoon oil and then the lychee syrup, chicken stock, soy sauce and cornflour. Mix well and cook for a few seconds. When thoroughly hot pour over the chicken balls and lychees and serve immediately.

CHICKEN WITH PEPPERS

dark meat of 1 chicken
8 water chestnuts
1 tablespoon cornflour
1 onion
SAUCE:
¾ cup chicken stock
2 tablespoons soy sauce

3 small sweet peppers
2 teaspoons soy sauce
1 tablespoon sherry
1 cup oil

1 tablespoon sherry
1 teaspoon cornflour

Cut the chicken meat into half inch cubes and mix with the soy sauce, cornflour and sherry. Heat a frying pan and add 4 tablespoons oil and when hot fry the chicken for 1 minute.

Cut the water chestnuts into cubes and slice the peppers and add to the chicken, frying all together for ten seconds. Remove and drain.

Reheat the pan and add 2 tablespoons oil. Mix the sauce ingredients and add to the pan. Bring to a boil, add the chicken and vegetables and cook for 1 minute more. Serve hot.

CHICKEN GIZZARDS

5 gizzards
6 water chestnuts
2 tablespoons oil
2 tablespoons soy sauce
½ teaspoon salt

1 small onion, sliced
1 bamboo shoot
2 teaspoons sherry
1 teaspoon chopped ginger
1 cup water

Slice the bamboo shoot and water chestnuts. Remove the fat, membrane and the inner skin of the gizzards and cut each one into 6 pieces.

Heat a frying pan and add the oil. When hot add the sliced gizzards, onion and ginger and sauté for a minute. Then add the salt, sherry and soy sauce and cook for 5 seconds. Add the water chestnuts, bamboo shoots and the water. Cover and simmer for 30 minutes. Serve hot.

CHICKEN WITH PEPPERS

4 *chicken legs*
10 *water chestnuts*
1 *onion*
1 *tablespoon cornflour*
6 *tablespoons oil*
SAUCE:
¾ *cup chicken stock*
2 *tablespoons soy sauce*

2 *red and 2 green sweet pepper*
2 *teaspoons soy sauce*
1 *tablespoon sherry*
¼ *teaspoon salt*

1 *tablespoon sherry*
1 *teaspoon cornflour*

Remove the meat from the bones and cut into pieces the size of half a walnut. Smear these pieces with a mixture of the soy sauce, cornflour and sherry. Heat a frying pan and add 4 tablespoons of oil. When hot fry the chicken and the sliced onion for 1 minute. Add the water chestnuts and the peppers, sliced, and fry with the chicken for 5 seconds. Remove and drain.

Reheat the pan, add 2 tablespoons of oil and the prepared sauce. Bring to a boil, add the chicken and the vegetables and simmer for 6 minutes. Serve immediately.

CHICKEN WITH TOMATOES

I *small chicken*
2 *tomatoes*
I *tablespoon soy sauce*
I *teaspoon cornflour*
SAUCE:
I *tablespoon soy sauce*
¼ *teaspoon salt*
I *teaspoon sugar*

I *onion, sliced*
6 *tablespoons oil*
I *tablespoon sherry*

I *tablespoon cornflour*
¼ *cup chicken stock*

Remove all meat from the chicken and cube it. Smear with a mixture of the soy sauce, sherry and cornflour. Heat a frying pan and add the oil. When hot add the onion and chicken and fry until the chicken begins to brown. Remove and drain. Reheat the pan and add 2 tablespoons of the oil and the blended sauce ingredients. Stir and when it boils add the tomatoes, cut into 8 pieces, the chicken and onion and fry together for 2 minutes. Serve immediately.

CHICKEN WITH VEGETABLES

breast of I *chicken*
½ *lb. shelled peas*
1½ *cups chicken stock*
½ *teaspoon salt*

2 *small cucumbers, sliced*
I *bamboo shoot, sliced*
I *tablespoon cornflour*
½ *cup oil*

Shred the chicken meat. Heat a frying pan, add the oil and when hot sauté the chicken for 5 seconds. Drain the chicken and put aside. Reheat the pan and add 2 tablespoons of the drained oil. When hot add the vegetables and sauté for 2 minutes. Add the stock and simmer for 5 minutes. Add the salt and cornflour mixed with a little water and simmer for 5 minutes more. Add the chicken and when it is warmed through serve immediately.

CANTON FRIED CHICKEN

1 *small chicken*
4 *tablespoons soy sauce*
2 *spring onions*
½ *cup water*
1 *tablespoon cornflour*

2 *tablespoons oil*
oil for deep frying
1 *teaspoon sherry*
1 *cup chicken stock*

Disjoint the chicken and rub it with a mixture of 2 tablespoons soy sauce and 2 tablespoons of oil. Put the oil in a deep fat frying pan and heat to almost 400 degrees. Put the chicken pieces in a wire basket and lower into the fat, reducing the flame at the same time. Remove the chicken when it is golden brown. (It can if you prefer be cooked in less fat, turning it until brown on both sides.)

Blend together 2 tablespoons soy sauce, ¼ cup water, 2 chopped onions and the sherry and put in a pan in which 2 tablespoons of oil have been heated. Add the chicken and cook over a low flame for 15 minutes or 20 if the chicken isn't quite tender. Remove the chicken and keep warm. Add to the pan the chicken stock, 1 tablespoon cornflour and ¼ cup water. Cook gently for a few minutes until the sauce thickens and then pour it over the chicken and serve immediately.

CHICKEN WITH BAMBOO SHOOTS

1 5-lb. chicken
2 large bamboo shoots
2 tablespoons sherry
4 tablespoons soy sauce
1½ cups water

2 spring onions
3 tablespoons oil
1 tablespoon sugar
ginger size of walnut, sliced

Wash the chicken, remove the legs and disjoint them. Halve the chicken down the back and then with a cleaver cut each half into four or five pieces. Cut the onions into inch lengths.

Heat a frying pan and add the oil. When it is hot add the chicken and fry for 5 minutes, turning constantly. Then add the water, soy sauce, sherry, ginger and onions. Cover the pan, turn the flame low and allow to simmer for 15 minutes. Add the sugar and the bamboo shoots, sliced. Cover the pan again and continue simmering for 5 or 6 minutes or until the chicken is tender. Serve hot.

CHICKEN OMELETTE

breast of 1 *chicken*   5 *egg whites*
1 *teaspoon cornflour*   ¼ *teaspoon salt*
SAUCE:
5 *tablespoons chicken stock* ¼ *teaspoon salt*
2 *teaspoons sherry*   ½ *teaspoon cornflour*

Pass the chicken meat through a mincer so that it is very fine indeed. With a fork mix the chicken smoothly with the unbeaten egg whites. Add the cornflour and salt and mix in thoroughly and then beat with a fork or an egg beater.

Heat a frying pan, add plenty of oil and when it is fairly hot —about 275 degrees—pour in the chicken and egg mixture and cook until the whole thing turns white. Turn it once while cooking so that both sides are equally done. Remove the chicken mixture and drain on absorbent paper.

Pour off the oil from the pan and add the chicken stock. When this boils put in the other sauce ingredients, first mixing the cornflour with a little water. Cook the sauce over gentle heat until it thickens. Return the chicken and egg mixture to the pan and cook gently for about 2 minutes. Serve immediately.

CHICKEN WITH LILY BUDS

1 *medium chicken*	12 *yellow lily buds*
6 *mushrooms*	½ *cup oil*
3 *cups water*	

SAUCE:

3 *tablespoons soy sauce*	2 *tablespoons sherry*
2 *teaspoons sugar*	½ *teaspoon salt*

Clean the chicken and smear it with the sauce mixture. Heat a deep frying pan and add the oil. When hot fry the chicken whole, browning slightly on all sides. Remove and drain.

Reheat the pan, add 2 tablespoons of oil and when hot fry the washed lily buds, which should not be bigger than two inches, and the mushrooms (whole), for 2 minutes. Return the chicken to the pan, add the water and cover. Simmer gently until the chicken is tender enough for the meat to be taken easily from the bones with chopsticks.

FRIED SPRING CHICKEN

2 *small spring chickens or* 1 *medium one*	½ *cup oil*
	1 *onion*
1 *cucumber*	1 *red pepper*
1 *tablespoon cornflour*	1 *tablespoon soy sauce*

SAUCE:

1 *tablespoon cornflour*	½ *teaspoon salt*
2 *tablespoons soy sauce*	½ *cup chicken stock*
½ *teaspoon sugar*	

Split the chickens or chicken in half and then each half in about three pieces, with bone. Mix 1 tablespoon cornflour and 1 tablespoon soy sauce in a basin and stir the chicken pieces in it until they are covered.

Mix the sauce ingredients and add to them the vegetables,

sliced. (Leave the cucumber skin on). Stir until the vegetables are well covered with the mixture. Heat a frying pan and add the oil. When it is hot fry the chicken until it is browned on all sides and is tender. Remove, drain and put on a warm dish. Reheat the pan and add 2 tablespoons of oil and when it is quite hot add the vegetables and fry briskly for 5 minutes. Pour them over the chicken and serve immediately.

CHICKEN WITH CELERY AND PINEAPPLE

1 *medium chicken*	1 *cup diced celery*
3 *slices pineapple*	1 *cup chicken stock*
3 *tablespoons oil*	1 *teaspoon salt*
$\frac{1}{2}$ *teaspoon sugar*	*dash pepper*
SAUCE:	
2 *tablespoons cornflour*	$\frac{1}{4}$ *cup water*
2 *teaspoons soy sauce*	

Put the chicken in a saucepan and cover with water. Boil until it is almost tender. Remove and drain. Boil the celery until almost tender and then drain. Heat a frying pan and add the oil. When hot add the salt and pepper. Add to this the chicken breast sliced, across the grain, in quarter inch slices. Cook till slightly brown then add the chicken stock, sugar, the pineapple slices cut into six pieces and the cooked celery. Cook for 5 seconds then add the sauce mixture and continue cooking until it thickens and the pineapple and celery are heated through. Serve immediately.

CANTONESE SALT CHICKEN

1 *small chicken*   2 *lb. kitchen salt*

Clean the chicken well and wipe the interior as dry as possible. Hang the chicken in a draught for an hour or two so that it dries thoroughly.

Put the salt into a deep iron pot, cover it and put over a moderate flame. When the salt is very hot make a hole in the centre of it and put the chicken, neck down, into the cavity. With a spoon pack the hot salt all round the bird so that only the rump end is visible. Cover the pot again and place over a low flame. Cook for 1 hour, remove the chicken and serve immediately.

SKEWERED CHICKEN

breast of 1 *chicken*   ½ *lb. sliced ham*
12 *small mushrooms*   4 *tablespoons oil*
SAUCE:
½ *teaspoon cornflour*   ½ *teaspoon salt*
1 *tablespoon sherry*

Slice the chicken breast in pieces about an eighth of an inch thick and soak them in the sauce mixture for 5 minutes. Cut the ham into pieces about the size of half-a-crown. On skewers put first a piece of chicken, then a small mushroom and then a piece of ham. Keep up this order until three or four short skewers are full. Then place in a flat dish with the oil and turn them until they are well covered with oil.

They are then roasted over an open fire for 8 to 10 minutes or roasted in a hot oven for about 10 minutes. Remove the skewers and serve immediately.

STUFFED CHICKEN

1 *medium chicken*	¾ *lb. pork (minced)*
3 *spring onions*	2 *teaspoons chopped ginger*
1 *tablespoon cornflour*	1 *tablespoon sherry*
1 *teaspoon salt*	½ *teaspoon sugar*
1 *tablespoon soy sauce*	½ *cup water*
¼ *cup oil*	

Boil the chicken in water for an hour and then bone it. This is done most easily by splitting the back. Mince the pork and chop the onions finely. Add to the pork and onions, the corn-flour, ginger, sherry, salt, sugar, soy sauce and enough of the water to make it all hang together. Stuff the chicken with this mixture and sew it up. Roast in a hot oven, putting the oil in the pan together with a little soy sauce, for 45 minutes or until it is tender.

Place the chicken on a serving dish and cut it into slices about half an inch thick. Serve while it is still hot.

FRIED CHICKEN WITH GINGER

1 *medium chicken*	2 *tablespoons sherry*
2 *tablespoons soy sauce*	3 *teaspoons cornflour*
½ *cup oil*	2 *teaspoons chopped ginger*

Boil the chicken for about an hour and then cut the meat from the bones and let it cool. Make a smooth mixture of the sherry, soy sauce, cornflour and ginger, which must be chopped very finely indeed. Cut the chicken meat into pieces of about a cubic inch and put in the sauce mixture. Let them soak for some minutes, stirring frequently.

Heat a frying pan and add the oil. When hot put in the chicken and fry over a brisk flame until the chicken is brown and crisp. Serve immediately.

This dish can also be made without the ginger if desired.

ROAST CHICKEN

1 *medium chicken*	*fresh ginger*
3 *spring onions*	1 *cup soy sauce*
½ *cup sherry*	1 *teaspoon salt*
1 *teaspoon sugar*	3-4 *cups water*

Put the water in a saucepan and add all the ingredients except the chicken, cutting the onions in two-inch lengths and using fresh ginger as big as two walnuts. Slice the ginger thickly.

When the water boils put the chicken in and boil for 15 minutes. Turn the flame out and let the chicken stand in the covered pot for another 15 minutes.

Remove the chicken and place in a roasting pan on a low rack. Roast in the oven for half an hour at about 450 degrees by which time the chicken should be well browned all over.

With a heavy knife cut the chicken in two through the back and then with a cleaver cut each half into five or six pieces, complete with bone. Arrange on a dish and serve immediately. In eating dip each piece into the pepper and salt mixture.

If you prefer the chicken can be carved more or less in the western manner, removing each half of the breast and cutting into about four pieces and the legs disjointed.

¶ DUCK

In cooking ducks in Chinese style there is one very important thing to remember. Chinese cooks always begin by removing the tail of the duck and with it the adjacent oil sacs. They want no oily taste detracting from the true flavour of the bird they prize above all others.

PEKING DUCK

1 *large duck*
1 *piece fresh ginger*
12 *spring onions*
2 *tablespoons oil*
PANCAKES:
5 *cups flour*
2 *cups water*

1 *onion*
thick soy sauce sometimes called Hiosin
salt and pepper to taste

1 *teaspoon salt*
¼ *cup oil*

This is one of the great Chinese dishes and was always on the banquet menu in Peking. It takes some time to prepare but the results are well worth the time and trouble. It is best to prepare the pancakes first.

Add the salt to the flour and then add 2 cups of boiling water, mixing as it goes in. Place the dough on a board and knead it well. Roll it out a quarter of an inch thick and cut into circles about half an inch in diameter. Smear a little oil on each side and dust with flour and then roll into pancake shape as thin as possible—as thin as paper if you can. Heat a pan, not too hot, and cook each pancake (without oil of any kind) until it is slightly browned on both sides. If you have a soapstone or other griddle for making American style pancakes—in other words a frying pan without sides—this is better than a frying pan. These pancakes, known in Peking as *Pao Ping*, are commonly called Peking doilies. Make three or four for each diner.

Now the duck. Clean it thoroughly so that not a pin feather

remains. Rub it well, breast and back, with salt and pepper. Clean the inside thoroughly and put inside a sliced onion and a few slices of ginger root.

Put 2 tablespoons of oil in a roasting pan and then the duck in the pan. Put it in an oven heated to 250 degrees and leave the duck for two hours. Remove from the oven and rub the breast and back with the Hiosin sauce and return the bird to the oven for another 30 minutes. Remove and add more Hiosin sauce and turn the duck upside down. Continue cooking for 15 or 20 minutes by which time the skin should be evenly brown and crisp, the fat under the skin crisp too. To ensure crisp fat under the skin some cooks blow in air between breast and skin before the cooking process starts.

When the duck is ready take a medium sized paring knife, very sharp, and take off the skin in pieces about two inches square. Be careful not to take the meat with it. In this dish the skin is the primary thing, the meat secondary. Serve the crisp skin on a warm dish immediately.

Place the doilies, warmed, on the table and also dishes containing more of the Hiosin sauce and the onions sliced lengthwise into quarters.

To eat, place a doily in the left hand and in the middle of it two pieces of duck skin, some Hiosin sauce and a piece of onion. Fold over the doily twice and eat while hot.

When the skin is exhausted the meat may be taken off in small pieces and eaten similarly.

DUCK WITH BAMBOO SHOOTS

1 *medium duck*   2 *bamboo shoots, sliced*
small piece ginger   1 *tablespoon sugar*
1 *teaspoon cornflour*   4 *tablespoons oil*
3 *tablespoons Hiosin sauce*   1 *onion, sliced*
4 *tablespoons soy sauce*   2 *tablespoons sherry*
1 *teaspoon salt*   1 *clove garlic*
3 *cups cold water*

Clean the duck well and with a heavy cleaver split it down the middle and then each half into four or five pieces. Smear it with a mixture of the Hiosin sauce, sugar, sherry, salt and cornflour. Let it stand in the mixture a few minutes.

Heat a frying pan and add the oil. When hot add the onion, garlic and the ginger, sliced. Fry for 5 seconds and then add the duck and fry until it is golden brown. Turn it fairly frequently. Then add the soy sauce and water and simmer for 20 minutes, covered. Add the bamboo shoots and continue cooking until the duck is tender.

JADE BELT DUCK

1 *duck*   1 *lb. sliced ham*
small piece ginger   2 *bunches leek leaves*
2 *tablespoons sherry*   3 *tablespoons soy sauce*
½ *teaspoon salt*   2 *cups water*

Clean the duck well and boil it in water for 15 minutes. Remove the duck and reserve the water. Remove the meat from the duck and cut in pieces about one inch by two. Wrap each piece in a piece of ham and tie together with the green leaf of a leek. Arrange these in a deep bowl or pot and add to them the water, sherry, soy sauce, salt and the ginger, chopped up finely. Place the bowl over a saucepan of boiling water and steam until the duck is tender, about an hour. Serve hot immediately.

PINEAPPLE DUCK I

1 *duck*
1 *clove garlic, chopped*
3 *cups cold water*
SAUCE:
4 *tablespoons soy sauce*
1 *tablespoon sugar*
1 *tablespoon finely chopped ginger*

4 *slices tinned pineapple*
½ *cup pineapple juice*
5 *tablespoons oil*

1 *teaspoon sherry*
½ *teaspoon salt*

Clean the duck and smear it well with the sauce mixture. Heat a deep frying pan and add the oil. When hot add the garlic and fry until it is brown. Add the duck and brown it on all sides. Transfer the contents of the pan to a deep roasting dish like a Dutch oven, after which add the water and pineapple juice. Cover and simmer until the duck is tender, which will be about an hour. Place the duck on a serving dish and keep warm. Cut each pineapple slice into four pieces and garnish the duck with them.

Add a little cornflour to the sauce in the pan and cook till it thickens, stirring all the time. Pour it over the duck and serve.

PINEAPPLE DUCK II

Proceed as in the above recipe but when the duck is cooked remove to a warm place, add the pieces of pineapple to the sauce and cook for 5 seconds.

Slice the breast meat of the duck across the grain in slices half an inch thick. Arrange these on a serving dish, a piece of duck and a piece of pineapple alternately. Pour the thickened sauce over duck and pineapple and serve immediately.

ROAST DUCK I

1 *duck*
4 *teaspoons honey*
¼ *cup chicken stock*

4 *teaspoons sugar*
1 *tablespoon soy sauce*
1 *teaspoon salt*

Mix well together the sugar, honey, soy sauce, salt and chicken stock. Clean the duck thoroughly and place in the mixture. Soak the duck for 40 minutes, turning frequently. Then place on a rack in a roasting pan with a little water in the pan and cook in a moderate oven for about an hour and three-quarters for a 5-lb. duck. Serve immediately.

ROAST DUCK II

1 *duck*
2 *spring onions*
1 *teaspoon salt*

1 *cup water*
1 *tablespoon sugar*

Rub the breast of the duck with the sugar and the salt. Cut the onions up and put with a sprinkle of salt and a cup of water into the interior of the duck, which should then be sewn up.

Place the duck on a rack in a roasting pan and, for a 5-lb. duck, cook for 45 minutes in a moderately hot oven. Then raise the temperature considerably for about 5 minutes to brown the skin, which should be crisp like crackling when the duck is served.

Roast ducks are not brought to the table whole but cut into convenient sections so that they can easily be taken with chopsticks. The legs and wings are cut into pieces, each side of the breast removed whole and then sliced across in pieces half an inch wide. The backbone is then laid on a serving dish, the legs and wings put more or less in their proper places and the breast meat laid in two rows down the middle. Serve immediately.

SALT DUCK

1 *medium duck*   1 *tablespoon salt*
1 *teaspoon pepper*   *water*

Salt duck, or salt-water duck is a favourite dish in the lower Yangtze valley and is served cold. Mix the salt and pepper and rub all over the duck, breast, back, legs and wings. Then rub some inside the duck. Then leave it in a cool place for two days. Before cooking rinse off the duck under a water tap for a moment to remove most of the salt and pepper. Put it in a large saucepan with 6 or 8 cups of water. Bring to a boil quickly then reduce the heat and simmer for 1 hour. Chill the duck and serve cold, carving it as for roast duck.

GINGER DUCKLING

1 *duckling*   1 *piece fresh ginger*
2 *tablespoons sherry*   1 *tablespoon cornflour*
2 *tablespoons soy sauce* 2 *tablespoons oil*
1 *spring onion*   *salt to taste*

Cut up the ginger finely, preferably shredding it on a grater. Take the meat from the breast of the duckling and from the legs. Shred the meat on a grater and soak it for a few minutes in a mixture of the sherry, cornflour, soy sauce, salt and chopped onion. Put 2 tablespoons of oil into a hot frying pan and when the oil is hot put in the duck meat, stirring constantly while cooking for about a minute. Then add the shredded ginger and cook, still stirring, for 3 minutes. Serve immediately.

THE EIGHT PRECIOUS DUCK

1 5-lb. duck
6 tablespoons soy sauce
1 tablespoon sugar
12 almonds
12 chestnuts
1 tablespoon raisins
fresh ginger size of a
    walnut

½ cup glutinous rice
4 spring onions
2 tablespoons pearl barley
12 lotus seeds
12 dates or other preserved
    fruits
3 tablespoons sherry
6 cups water

Boil the rice and pearl barley together in two cups of water for half an hour over moderate flame. Drain and mix with it 2 tablespoons soy sauce, 1 teaspoon sugar, one chopped onion, the almonds, chestnuts, dates, lotus seeds and raisins. Stuff the cleaned duck with this mixture and sew it up. Put the stuffed duck in a saucepan with three or four cups of water and add to it the rest of the soy sauce, the sherry and the onions and ginger. Bring quickly to a boil, then turn the flame low and simmer for not less than 50 minutes. Turn the duck over, add the rest of the sugar to the water and simmer until the duck is tender, which should be about an hour.

This duck can be eaten either hot or cold. Remove the stuffing and make a bed of it on a serving dish. Carve the duck as for roast duck and arrange attractively on the bed of stuffing.

STEWED DUCK WITH ONION

1 *large duck*   12 *spring onions*
8 *tablespoons soy sauce*   2 *teaspoons sugar*
3 *tablespoons sherry*   *fresh ginger size of an egg*

Chop the onions in three-inch lengths, pour over them 2 tablespoons of soy sauce and a little sugar and stuff them inside the duck. Put the duck in a saucepan with three or four cups of water to which should be added the rest of the soy sauce, the sherry and the ginger cut into thin slices. Bring to a boil and then simmer for about an hour. Turn the duck over, add the rest of the sugar and continue simmering until the duck is very tender, at least another hour.

   This duck is usually served whole and is so tender the meat can easily be taken from the bones with chopsticks.

STUFFED DUCK

1 *medium duck*	10 *water chestnuts*
1 *bamboo shoot*	6 *mushrooms*
¼ *lb. fresh pork*	¼ *lb. ham*
12 *lotus seeds or other nuts*	*small piece ginger*
2 *tablespoons soy sauce*	½ *cup chicken stock*
1 *teaspoon sugar*	1 *tablespoon sherry*
salt to taste	3 *tablespoons oil*
	1 *cup cooked rice*

Remove the breast bones of the duck from the opening at the neck. Heat a frying pan and add 2 tablespoons of oil. When hot sauté the pork, cubed, the mushrooms, sliced, the ham, cubed, and the nuts. After 2 or 3 minutes add the chicken stock, soy sauce, sherry, salt, sugar, ginger, rice, and 1 tablespoon of oil. Simmer for 30 seconds.

Remove this from the pan and mix thoroughly. Stuff the duck and sew up both openings. Place in a large bowl and steam the duck for at least an hour and a half or until tender.

This can either be carved in the kitchen for serving or by the host at the table.

If they are available use that cereal product known as Job's Tears instead of rice. If they are used you need a third of a cup of them and they should be soaked in water for 2 hours and then put in the pan to sauté with the pork, ham, etc.

DUCK WITH ALMONDS

1 *medium duck*
½ *cup diced bamboo shoot*
1 *cup Chinese or other cabbage*
1 *teaspoon salt*
1 *tablespoon sherry*
4 *tablespoons oil*

1 *cup diced celery*
1 *cup water chestnuts, sliced*
½ *cup blanched almonds*
1 *cup chicken stock*
1 *tablespoon soy sauce*
1 *tablespoon cornflour*
3 *tablespoons stock*

Cube the bamboo shoot and cut the celery into pieces an inch long. If Chinese cabbage isn't available use Swiss chard and if that isn't available ordinary cabbage will do. Cut across the cabbage or chard in three-quarter inch slices until you have enough to fill a cup tightly packed.

Remove the breast of the duck in two pieces and slice it across the grain in pieces a quarter of an inch thick. Marinate the duck in a mixture of the soy sauce and sherry.

Put one tablespoon of oil into a hot frying pan and fry the blanched almonds until they begin to turn golden then remove and drain. Add the rest of the oil to the pan and when hot fry the duck meat until it turns a golden brown. Remove it, drain and place with the almonds.

Into what oil remains in the pan put the vegetables and fry over a moderate flame for 3 minutes, turning occasionally. Then add the cup of stock and the salt, cover the pan and simmer for 5 minutes. Remove the lid and add the duck and almonds. Re-cover and continue simmering for 3 minutes. Remove the pan from the fire and when the liquid ceases to boil add the cornflour and stock which should be mixed with what remains of the marinating mixture. Return to the fire and stir constantly until the sauce thickens. Serve immediately.

STEWED DUCK

1 *medium duck*　　　　　　1 *spring onion*
½ *cup soy sauce*　　　　　3 *tablespoons sherry*
1 *cup chicken stock*　　　2 *cups water*
2 *teaspoons sugar*　　　　*salt to taste*

Wash the duck and put into a large pot with the stock and the water. Bring to a boil and then add the soy sauce, sherry, salt and chopped onion. Cover and simmer for 1 hour. Turn the duck over, add the sugar and simmer for 1 hour more. By this time the meat should come away from the bones easily. If not simmer it further.

Serve in a dish with the sauce from the pot. It should be possible to pull the meat off the duck with chopsticks.

PEKING SWEET DUCK

1 *large fat duck*　　　　　½ *cup honey*
20 *Peking doilies, see page* 53　10 *spring onions split in four*
sweetened soy bean paste

The duck is cleaned and air is pumped in under the skin of the breast. It is then hung up in a draught for a few hours until it is thoroughly dry. The duck is then coated with the honey and turned slowly over the hot embers of a fire until the skin is a deep golden brown and crisp and the fat underneath crisp with it. Broken charcoal and charcoal powder can be added to the fire from time to time to keep it going at the same heat. This toasting process will take at least 1 hour.

With a sharp knife cut off the crisp skin and fat in pieces about two square inches in size. Serve on a warm dish. The duck is eaten as is Peking duck. Two pieces are put on a Peking doily, a piece or two of onion, raw, added, and some soy paste or thick sauce. Then fold over the doily and eat. The breast meat can then be sliced off in small pieces and eaten in the same way.

C

FRIED DUCK

1 *medium duck*	2 *eggs*
4 *tablespoons cornflour*	2 *tablespoons soy sauce*
1 *tablespoon sherry*	1 *spring onion*
3 *slices fresh ginger*	½ *teaspoon salt*
3 *tablespoons oil*	4 *tablespoons water*

The duck should be of sufficient size so that the breast and legs when removed weigh about 2 lbs. Mix the soy sauce, sherry, chopped onion and chopped ginger in a bowl and let the four pieces of duck marinate for half an hour, turning them occasionally. Mix the eggs, cornflour, salt and water together into a paste and coat each piece of duck with it liberally.

Heat a frying pan, add the oil and when it is hot fry the duck 3 minutes on each side over a fierce flame. Then turn the flame to low and cook for 15 minutes at least or until the skin of the duck is crisp. Turn it occasionally so that both sides get equally cooked.

Remove from the fire, slice the duck into slices half an inch thick, arrange on a dish and serve immediately.

PINEAPPLE AND GINGER DUCK

1 *duckling* (4 *lbs.*)	1 *tin sliced pineapple*
½ *cup preserved ginger*	1 *teaspoon salt*
SAUCE:	
1 *tablespoon cornflour*	3 *tablespoons ginger syrup*
1 *cup pineapple juice*	

Steam the duckling until the breast is tender, about two hours or a little more. Remove the skin from the breast and then remove the two sides of the breast and place side by side on a dish. Slice across the breast meat so that the slices are half an inch wide or a little more. Cut the slices of pineapple into quarters and arrange round the duck. Cut the ginger into thin slices and arrange on the duck meat. Keep in a warm place.

Heat the pineapple juice and ginger syrup in a frying pan and then add the cornflour mixed with a little water. Continue cooking, stirring constantly, until the sauce thickens, then pour it over the duck and serve immediately.

DUCK WITH RED SAUCE

1 *duckling* (3 *to* 4 *lbs.*)
3 *spring onions*
4 *mushrooms*
2 *teaspoons salt*
3 *tablespoons soy sauce*

fresh ginger the size of a walnut
2 *teaspoons sesame oil*
2 *tablespoons sherry*
2 *teaspoons sugar*

Put the duck in a saucepan and add to it all the other ingredients, slicing the ginger finely and quartering the mushrooms and chopping the onions into two-inch lengths. Then add enough water to cover the duck. Bring it to a boil and then simmer until the duck is quite tender, which will be an hour and a half or more. The breast meat must be tender enough to tear apart with chopsticks. Place the duck in a large serving dish and pour over it the liquid contents of the saucepan. Serve immediately.

FRIED WILD DUCK

2 *wild ducks*	4 *mushrooms*
1 *bamboo shoot*	5 *tablespoons oil*
1 *teaspoon cornflour*	1 *teaspoon sugar*
1 *tablespoon sherry*	*salt and pepper*

Remove the breast of both ducks and slice about a quarter of an inch thick. Dust them with salt and pepper and then roll them in the cornflour mixed with a little water. Heat a frying pan and add the oil. When it is hot fry the duck meat over a brisk flame for 2 minutes. Remove and place to one side. Into the oil that remains in the frying pan put the mushrooms, sliced, and the bamboo shoot, sliced, with the sugar and a little salt. Fry over a brisk flame for 3 minutes. Return the duck to the pan with the vegetables and add the sherry. Turn the flame down and continue cooking for 1 minute. Serve immediately.

¶ PIGEON

FRIED SQUAB

2 *pigeons*
2 *cups oil*
2 *teaspoons salt*
1 *onion, sliced*

3 *tablespoons soy sauce*
2 *teaspoons sugar*
1 *tablespoon sherry*
1 *tablespoon chopped ginger*

Clean the pigeons thoroughly and with a cleaver cut them into halves and then each half into three pieces, with the bone attached. Marinate them in a mixture of the soy sauce, salt, sherry and sugar for about 10 minutes. Then add the sliced onion and chopped ginger and allow to stand for 2 hours.

Heat a frying pan and add the oil. When it is hot fry the pigeons until they are brown, then drain and serve immediately.

BRAISED PIGEON EGGS

8 *pigeon eggs*
2 *mushrooms, sliced*
2 *cups oil*
SAUCE:
4 *tablespoons soy sauce*
1 *teaspoon sugar*

1 *bamboo shoot, sliced*
½ *cup flour*

1 *tablespoon sherry*
1 *teaspoon cornflour*

Boil the eggs for 5 minutes and remove the shells. Then boil the bamboo shoot and mushrooms for 5 minutes. Soak the cooked eggs in the sauce mixture for a few minutes then remove and roll in the flour. Heat a frying pan and add the oil. When hot fry the eggs until they are brown then remove and drain. Reheat the pan and add 3 tablespoons of oil. Put in the bamboo shoots, mushrooms and the sauce mixture. Lastly add the eggs and simmer for ten seconds. Serve hot.

MINCED PIGEON

2 *pigeons*
2 *stalks celery*
4 *mushrooms*
6 *tablespoons oil*
½ *cup chicken stock*
2 *tablespoons sherry*
salt

1 *onion*
6 *water chestnuts*
bamboo shoots
3 *tablespoons soy sauce*
1 *tablespoon cornflour*
1 *tablespoon sugar*

Remove all meat from the pigeons and cut into quarter inch cubes. Then dice the onion, celery, water chestnuts, mushrooms and enough bamboo shoots to make half a cupful.

Put 2 tablespoons oil into a heated frying pan and sauté the pigeon meat for 1 minute and then remove it. Add two more tablespoons of oil to the pan and when hot quickly sauté the vegetables—about 5 seconds. Then add the soy sauce, sugar, salt to taste and the chicken stock. Let the whole thing simmer for a minute and then add the cornflour mixed in a very little water, about 2 tablespoons. Add the pigeon and cook the whole thing for not more than 15 seconds. Make a bed of shredded lettuce on a serving dish and pour the whole thing over the lettuce and serve at once.

POACHED PIGEON EGGS

4 mushrooms
1 bamboo shoot
¼ cup chicken stock
¼ lb. chard or celery cab-
    bage
saltspoon salt

10 pigeon eggs
¼ cup cubed ham
1 tablespoon cornflour
4 teaspoons soy sauce
½ teaspoon sugar
4 tablespoons oil

The mushrooms can be either fresh or dried. If dried soak for 30 minutes. Slice the mushrooms and the bamboo shoot and cut the chard or cabbage coarsely. Heat a frying pan, add 2 tablespoons of oil and when hot sauté the chard for 5 minutes. Then add the sugar and salt and cook for another 30 seconds. Then add the mushrooms, bamboo shoot and the ham, the chicken stock, the soy sauce and the cornflour mixed in a little water. Cook for 2 minutes, stirring constantly.

Put the vegetables and ham on a serving dish and keep warm. To the sauce in the pan add 2 tablespoons of oil and when it is thoroughly mixed into the sauce break the eggs carefully and drop one by one into the sauce. Cook them until the whites are set and then arrange them on the vegetables and ham. It is better to cook the eggs two at a time. Serve immediately.

BOILED PIGEON EGGS

Pigeon eggs are regarded as a great delicacy in China and are often added to clear soups. Boil them for 5 minutes, remove the shells and add one to each basin of soup, whether chicken or meat soup.

PIGEON WITH WATER CHESTNUTS

3 *young pigeons*
2 *spring onions*
¼ *cup chicken stock*
2 *tablespoons soy sauce*
½ *teaspoon sugar*
¼ *cup oil*

1 *egg*
15 *water chestnuts*
1 *tablespoon cornflour*
1 *tablespoon sherry*
salt to taste

Cut the pigeons in half down the middle and then with a cleaver cut each half into three pieces, with the bone. Beat the white of the egg lightly and add to it 1 teaspoon of cornflour. Let the pieces of pigeon stand in this a few minutes. Then heat a frying pan, add 4 tablespoons of oil and when hot sauté the pigeon for three minutes. Remove pigeon and keep warm.

Add another tablespoon or two of oil to the pan and put in the onions cut into inch lengths and also the water chestnuts, sliced. Cook for 2 minutes. Then add the chicken stock, the sherry, the soy sauce and the rest of the cornflour mixed in 2 tablespoons of water. Then add sugar, salt and a dash of pepper. Cook for 2 minutes more, add the pigeon and cook for a minute or two until the sauce thickens a little. Serve hot.

¶ PHEASANT

PHEASANT WITH RICE

1 *cup cubed cooked pheasant*	4 *eggs*
2 *spring onions*	*salt and pepper to taste*
4 *cups cooked rice*	2 *tablespoons diced ham*
2 *ozs. raisins*	6 *tablespoons oil*

Beat together four yolks and two whites of egg with half a teaspoon of salt and a dash of pepper. Chop the onions finely and add them to the eggs and beat again until the onions are well distributed in the mixture.

Heat frying pan, add 3 tablespoons of oil and when it is hot add the egg mixture and cook for 2 minutes, stirring constantly. Remove the egg and put in a dish.

Put 1 tablespoon of oil in the pan and when hot add the cooked rice and sauté for 5 or 6 minutes. Then add the eggs (which will have the consistency of buttered eggs) and mix well with the rice. Then add 2 tablespoons of oil, the pheasant meat, the ham and the raisins which should be soaked so that they swell up. Sauté the whole mixture over a moderate flame for 3 or 4 minutes, stirring constantly, and serve hot.

BRAISED PHEASANT

1 *pheasant*
2 *tablespoons oil*
1 *teaspoon sugar*
3 *slices ginger*

1 *spring onion*
1 *cup chicken stock*
2 *tablespoons sherry*

Wash the pheasant, a small one, split it down the middle and then with a cleaver cut each half into four or five sections complete with bone. Heat a frying pan and add the oil. When hot put the pheasant in and cook, stirring, for 5 minutes. Then add the stock, soy sauce, sherry, ginger and the onion cut into inch sections.

Cover the pan and turn the flame low. Simmer for 30 minutes, then add the sugar and cook for another 10 minutes. Serve immediately.

¶ TURKEY

ROAST TURKEY

1 *small turkey* (10 *lbs.*)	3 *cups soy sauce*
1 *cup sherry*	2 *tablespoons sugar*
fresh ginger	4 *spring onions*
1 *tablespoon salt*	*salt spoon of pepper*

Put about ten cups of water in a large saucepan and add the soy sauce, sherry, sugar, salt, pepper, onions (leaves as well) and half a dozen slices of fresh ginger. When it boils put the turkey in, cover and boil for 45 minutes.

Remove the turkey from the saucepan and place in a roasting pan with two cupfuls of the sauce from the saucepan. To this add 1 tablespoon of sesame oil.

Cook the turkey at about 450 degrees for an hour and a quarter, basting fairly often. If necessary turn up the heat towards the end to brown the bird thoroughly.

To serve, remove the two sides of the breast whole, then slice across the grain into slices a quarter of an inch thick. Arrange a bed of shredded lettuce on a warm serving dish and arrange the turkey meat on it in the form it would be on the bird.

SOUPS

SOUP STOCKS

There are two basic soup stocks in Chinese cookery but in these modern days many a Chinese cook takes a short cut by buying prepared stock in tins. Many of these are good but cannot, of course, equal stock made freshly in the kitchen.

MEAT STOCK

1 *lb. lean pork or beef*
3 *tablespoons chopped shrimp*
  or prawns
1 *teaspoon salt*

7 *cups cold water*
2 *teaspoons soy sauce*
½ *teaspoon sesame oil*

Slice or shred the meat and put in a saucepan with the shrimp or prawns and the water. Bring to a boil and simmer for 30 minutes. Then add whatever vegetables you wish, chopped or diced, and continue boiling for 10 minutes. Then add the soy sauce, salt and oil and cook for 2 minutes more. Pour through a wire sieve fine enough to prevent meat and vegetables going through.

CHICKEN STOCK

1 *large chicken*
7 *cups cold water*
½ *teaspoon salt*

½ *lb. pork*
2 *teaspoons soy sauce*

Put the chicken, whole, in a pot with the water and boil for 10 minutes, then reduce the flame and simmer for another 40

74

minutes. Remove the chicken and add the soy sauce, salt, and whatever vegetables you wish, either chopped or diced, and boil for 5 minutes more. Strain as above.

In making these stocks the Chinese put in a variety of vegetables, whatever happens to be on hand, including celery cabbage, bamboo shoot, water chestnut, celery, mustard greens, mushrooms, spinach.

Either of the above stocks can be used as vegetable soup immediately by serving as they come from the saucepan or they can be strained and reserved for use in the various soups.

In Chinese cookery thick and heavy soups are unknown with the exception of bird's nest soup—but that, of course, ranks with epicures as a principal dish rather than a soup. Generally soups are not served at the beginning of a meal but two soups may be served during the course of a banquet. Most Chinese soups are very light and delicate and their main purpose seems to be to clear the palate after several dishes (some of which may be quite pungent) before the next set of courses appear on the table. But most westerners eating Chinese food in their own houses, or even in Chinese restaurants, seem to prefer to have their Chinese soup where they would have it in their own cookery, at the beginning of the meal.

WON TON SOUP

½ lb. pork or beef
2 spring onions
1 cup spinach, tightly packed
1 egg

4 cups chicken broth
½ cup chopped celery
1½ cups flour
1½ teaspoons salt

Put the flour in a mixing bowl and add the egg, slightly beaten, then 2 tablespoons of water and mix thoroughly. Knead the dough on a pastry board until it is very smooth. Let it stand for 10 minutes and then roll out as thin as possible and cut it into three-inch squares. Chop the meat very finely and add ½ teaspoon salt, a dash of pepper and the onions, finely chopped. Mix this thoroughly and put a teaspoonful on each of the dough squares. Fold over diagonally and press the edges together so that the filling is well sealed in. Cook these in boiling salted water for 15 minutes and then remove and drain. Keep warm.

Then put the chicken broth in a saucepan and add the finely chopped celery. Cook for five minutes over a moderate flame and then add the spinach after removing the stems. Cook for 1 minute more and then pour the soup over the *won ton* as they are called. Serve immediately.

WATERCRESS SOUP

½ lb. lean pork
¼ cup diced celery
2 cups chicken stock
2 cups water

1 cup tightly packed watercress
1 small onion
1 teaspoon salt

Dice the pork and put in a saucepan with the water and salt. Add 1 tablespoon of finely chopped onion, the celery and the chicken stock and simmer, covered, for 20 minutes.

Lastly add the watercress, bring to a boil quickly and serve immediately.

CHICKEN MUSHROOM SOUP

4 cups chicken stock
1 tablespoon chopped onion
¼ cup diced celery

1 oz. egg noodles
4 large mushrooms

Put the broth in a saucepan and add the onion and celery.
Bring to a boil and then add the sliced mushrooms and the
noodles. Cook for 10 minutes and serve immediately.

CHICKEN SOUP

1 medium chicken
3 mushrooms
2 teaspoons soy sauce
8 cups water

¼ lb. lean ham
1 bamboo shoot
2 teaspoons salt

Wash the chicken and put in a large saucepan with the 8 cups
of water. Bring to the boil and add the mushrooms, whole, and
the bamboo shoot, sliced, and simmer for 45 minutes, covered.
Remove the chicken and take off the white meat in thin slices.
Return these to the saucepan and with them the ham,
shredded, the salt and the soy sauce. Simmer for another 20
minutes and serve immediately.

EGG SOUP

3 eggs
1 teaspoon soy sauce

2 cups chicken stock
½ teaspoon salt

Heat the stock in a saucepan and then add the eggs, beaten,
stirring constantly as they are poured slowly in. Then add soy
sauce and salt and cook gently until the egg appears to be
cooked. Serve immediately.

BIRD'S NEST SOUP

1 *chicken*
½ *lb. white bird's nest*
2 *tablespoons finely chopped ham*

2 *egg whites*
1 *teaspoon salt*
little chopped parsley
little cornflour

In Cantonese shops one can usually get either the real bird's nest or a gelatine substitute. Remove the breast of the chicken and prepare as for Chicken Velvet (see page 32), pounding with a cleaver and when mushy adding cornflour, salt and unbeaten egg whites. Soak the bird's nest in four cups of cold water for an hour. Then wash it carefully and put in a saucepan with three cups of cold water and simmer for half an hour. Drain.

Add the drained bird's nest to 4 cups of chicken stock made from the rest of the chicken and simmer for 20 minutes.

Remove from the fire and stir into it the prepared chicken velvet. Stir well, reheat for a few seconds, adding the chopped ham, salt and parsley. Pour into a soup dish and serve hot.

CELERY CABBAGE SOUP

1 *chicken carcass*
3 *cups celery cabbage*
2 *teaspoons soy sauce*
1 *tablespoon sherry*

7 *cups cold water*
½ *lb. pork, chopped small*
1 *teaspoon salt*
1 *tablespoon cornflour*

Break up the chicken carcass and put in a saucepan with 7 cups of cold water and bring to a boil. Then add the celery cabbage and simmer for 25 minutes. During this time mix the chopped meat with the sherry and the cornflour and at the end of the 25 minutes put pork balls, soy sauce and salt in the soup, after removing the chicken bones. Simmer for 15 minutes more to cook the pork balls and serve immediately.

If celery cabbage is not available ordinary cabbage can be

used instead, or for that matter any leafy vegetable. 'A cup' of cabbage means chopped and packed tight.

LOTUS ROOT SOUP

1 *small tin lotus root*
6 *dates*
saltspoon of salt

½ *lb. beef, sliced*
1 *tablespoon soy sauce*
6 *cups water*

Slice the lotus root thinly and put it with the sliced beef and the dates in cold water. Bring to the boil and continue to boil for five seconds. Then reduce the flame and allow it to simmer for at least 30 minutes. Add the salt just before serving.

MUSTARD GREENS SOUP

½ *lb. lean pork*
3 *cups mustard greens,*
  tightly packed
7 *cups cold water*

several chicken bones
2 *teaspoons soy sauce*
1 *teaspoon salt*

Put the pork, sliced thinly, chicken bones and cold water in a saucepan and bring to the boil. Turn down flame and simmer for 30 minutes. Then add the mustard greens after cutting the stalks into one-inch pieces. Boil for 2 or 3 minutes (uncovered so as to retain the fresh green of the vegetable) and add the soy sauce and salt just before serving.

CUCUMBER SOUP

1 *cucumber*
½ *tablespoon cornflour*
2 *tablespoons soy sauce*
7 *cups water*

½ *lb. pork*
1 *tablespoon sherry*
½ *teaspoon salt*

Peel and slice the cucumber. Cut the meat in thin slices and mix it in a basin with the sherry, cornflour and 1 tablespoon of soy sauce. Bring the cold water to a boil and add the other tablespoon of soy sauce. Then add the cucumber slices and boil for 1 minute. Then add the pork and continue to boil for 2 or 3 minutes. If the meat is cut thin enough this should of ample time to cook it. Add the salt just before serving.

MUSHROOM SOUP

This is made in exactly the same way as Cucumber Soup except that half a pound of fresh mushrooms, sliced, is used instead be the cucumber.

HAM AND MELON SOUP

½ *lb. ham*
7 *cups of water*

1 *lb. melon or vegetable marrow*

If there is a piece of ham bone handy, so much the better. Peel off the skin of the melon or marrow and cut the flesh into pieces half an inch thick and one inch square. Put these pieces and the ham into 7 cups of cold water. Bring to the boil over a fierce flame, then turn down the flame but keep the soup boiling for 30 minutes. Then remove the ham and cut the lean of it into small cubes. Return to soup and cook 5 minutes more. Add a little salt if it needs it (depending on the saltiness of the ham) and serve immediately.

FISH SOUP

1 *lb. filleted haddock*
1 *tablespoon sherry*
2 *tablespoons soy sauce*

1 *teaspoon salt*
1 *tablespoon cornflour*
1 *small onion*

Cut the fish into one-inch squares and put it in a mixture of the sherry, cornflour and 1 tablespoon of soy sauce. Slice the onion and put it with 1 teaspoon salt and 1 tablespoon of soy sauce in 7 cups of water and bring to the boil and then add the fish. Simmer, uncovered, for 5 minutes and serve hot.

DUCK SOUP I

carcass of a duck
1 *bamboo shoot*
1 *spring onion*
8 *cups water*

$\frac{1}{2}$ *lb. ham*
6 *mushrooms*
1 *teaspoon salt*

This is good to make after one has used the breast of a duck for some other dish. Cut the carcass into pieces and put it in 8 cups of water and bring to the boil. If any fat rises skim off as much as possible. Turn the flame low and add the ham in one piece, the onion whole and the bamboo shoot and mushrooms sliced. Simmer the whole for about an hour. Remove the bones and the ham. Dice the lean parts of the ham and return to the soup. Add the salt, simmer for 5 minutes more and serve.

DUCK SOUP II

This is less of a soup in the Chinese style and more of a principal dish. Proceed in the same way as above but use a duckling which must, of course, be boiled longer, at least an hour and a half.

At the end the duck is placed whole in a large serving dish, swimming in the soup and vegetables and the ham sliced and laid across the breast. The duck should be so tender that the breast meat can be removed easily with chopsticks.

CELESTIAL SOUP

The name of this soup indicates not that it is a supreme soup but that it is so 'light' it can be taken by the spirits or gods. It is sometimes called Soup of the Gods. It is seldom served as a soup but in a soup bowl as a drink to accompany very rich dishes. In other words it is to clear the palate.

2 *garlic cloves*	1 *spring onion*
2 *tablespoons soy sauce*	1 *teaspoon sesame oil*
1 *teaspoon salt*	6 *cups water*

Chop the garlic and the onion and mix with the sesame oil, salt and soy sauce. Bring the water to a brisk boil and add the other ingredients. Boil for 5 seconds, strain and serve.

CHICKEN SOUP

This is a basic chicken soup which can be made and reserved as stock or used immediately as a clear consommé. Like stocks in European cooking it is made mostly from odds and ends but as many ingredients as possible should go in.

Take chicken wings and bones, and if possible a carcass

chopped up, chicken feet which have been cleaned and skinned, gizzards cut in pieces and half a pound of pork bones, preferably rib bones. Cover these with cold water in a large saucepan, bring to a boil and boil for three or four minutes.

Discard the liquid and add to the pot a small piece of well cured ham, half a pound of sliced bamboo shoots, a little sliced ginger, two chopped spring onions, a tablespoon sherry and two quarts of cold water. Bring this to a boil under cover and then turn the flame low and simmer for at least 2 hours. Drain off the liquid.

CREAM OF CRAB SOUP

½ *cup crab meat*
2 *slices ginger*
2 *egg whites*
4 *cups chicken broth*
4 *tablespoons oil*

1 *spring onion*
1 *tablespoon sherry*
4 *tablespoons cream*
2 *teaspoons cornflour*

Heat a frying pan and add the oil and fry the ginger and the onion, chopped, for 1 minute. Add the crabmeat, salt to taste and the sherry and fry for 1 minute more. Then add the chicken broth after discarding the ginger. Bring to a boil.

Mix the egg whites, beaten but not stiff, the cream, 2 tablespoons of the chicken stock and the cornflour. Add this to the pan slowly, stirring constantly. Continue to cook gently for 2 or 3 minutes and serve immediately.

MUSHROOM SOUP

10 *mushrooms*	1 *bamboo shoot*
6 *water chestnuts*	4 *ozs. ham*
8 *ozs. pork*	4 *cups water*
1 *teaspoon salt*	

Slice the pork and add to the four cups of water brought to the boil. Cook for 3 or 4 minutes. Then add the mushrooms, sliced, the water chestnuts, quartered, and the bamboo shoot, sliced. Cover the pot and simmer for half an hour. Add the ham, shredded, and salt, and continue simmering for 10 minutes.

Pour all into a soup tureen and serve.

TURNIP SOUP

½ *lb. pork*	2 *white turnips*
1 *tablespoon soy sauce*	½ *teaspoon salt*
chicken bones	4 *cups water*

Make this when serving a chicken dish. Bring the water to a boil and add a chicken carcass. Then add the pork in one piece and the turnips cut to resemble orange segments. Simmer, covered, for at least half an hour then add soy sauce and salt and continue simmering for 5 minutes.

GREEN PEA SOUP WITH EGG

4 *cups beef stock*   1 *cup shelled peas*
2 *eggs*

Heat the beef stock and when at simmering heat add the shelled peas and cook for 7 minutes, by which time the peas should be tender. Beat the eggs slightly, bring the soup to the boil and slowly pour in the eggs, stirring constantly for 2 minutes by which time the egg should be separated into shreds.

HAM AND CABBAGE SOUP

1 *lb. ham*   1 *lb. of cabbage or celery*
8 *cups water*   *cabbage*
1 *tablespoon soy sauce*   *salt to taste*

If possible have some bone in the ham. Bring the water to a boil and put in the ham. Turn down the flame and simmer for 25 minutes. If European cabbage is used cut it in one inch 'rounds' and then quarter. If celery cabbage is used cut across in one inch slices. Add the cabbage to the soup together with soy sauce and salt and cook for 6 or 7 minutes. Remove the ham, cube the meat and discard the bone. Return the ham to the soup. Bring it to simmering heat and serve.

LEFT-OVER SOUP

2 cups left-over soup, beef,   ½ cup bamboo shoot
chicken or ham or mixed   ½ cup ham
½ cup chicken meat

Shred the ham and chicken and cut the bamboo shoot into cubes. Bring the soup to simmering point and add the meat and vegetable and simmer gently for 10 minutes.

Almost any meat and vegetable left-overs can be used in this soup and a tablespoon of soy sauce can always be added if desired.

RICE CHOWDER

3 lbs. beef bones   ½ lb. pork
4 spring onions   1½ cups rice
12 cups water   3 tablespoons soy sauce
2 teaspoons salt

Put the soup bones in the water when it boils and simmer them for an hour and a half. Remove them and add to the water the pork meat, diced, and the rice, which should have been washed three or four times in cold water. Simmer uncovered for about 2 hours. Cut the onions, including the leaves, into pieces an inch long and add to the chowder together with soy sauce and salt. Continue simmering for at least 15 minutes. Serve hot.

MUSHROOM SOUP

½ chicken   ½ lb. mushrooms
2 teaspoons salt   2 spring onions or 1 leek
1 tablespoon sherry   fresh ginger
6 cups water

With a cleaver chop the chicken into three or four pieces and add to the water together with the onions or leek cut in half, the mushrooms whole and the other ingredients. Simmer slowly for about 2 hours. Remove the chicken and the onions and serve.

MUSHROOM AND BEAN CURD SOUP

8 *mushrooms* $\frac{1}{4}$ *lb. bean curd*
1 *teaspoon salt*   4 *cups chicken stock*

Wash the mushrooms, cut them in half and put in a saucepan with the chicken stock. Bring to a boil and then simmer for about six minutes. Then add the bean curd, cut into cubes, and the salt. Continue simmering until the bean curd is heated through and serve.

CHICKEN CUCUMBER SOUP

1 *chicken (small)*   1 *small cucumber*
1 *teaspoon salt*   1 *teaspoon cornflour*
5 *cups water*

Remove the breast meat from the chicken and simmer the rest of the carcass in the water for about 2 hours. Remove the chicken and strain the stock to get it clear. Return the stock to the saucepan, and add the salt and the cucumber, sliced. Slice the chicken breast across the grain in slices about a quarter of an inch thick. Roll them in the cornflour and add to the saucepan. Bring to a boil and simmer for 5 minutes and serve.

¶ PORK

SWEET AND SOUR PORK

1 *lb. lean pork*
3 *slices pineapple*
2 *tablespoons flour*
½ *cup chicken broth*
dash pepper
SAUCE:
2½ *tablespoons cornflour*
2 *teaspoons soy sauce*
½ *cup vinegar*

3 *green peppers*
1 *egg*
1 *clove garlic*
1½ *teaspoons salt*
¾ *cup oil*

½ *cup honey or sugar*
⅔ *cup chicken broth*

Cut each pepper into eight or ten pieces and boil in water until about half cooked—about 4 minutes. Into a hot frying pan put the oil and 1 teaspoon salt. When hot add the chopped garlic and cook for a minute. Make a batter of the beaten egg, the flour and half a teaspoon of salt. Cut the pork into ¾ inch cubes and coat them thoroughly with the batter. Drop the cubes into the heated oil and sauté until golden brown.

Pour off the oil and then return 1 tablespoon to the pan and add to the pork the peppers, the pineapple slices cut into six pieces each and one third of a cup of chicken broth. Cover the pan and cook gently for 10 minutes.

Blend together all the sauce ingredients and add to the pan. Cook gently, stirring constantly, until the sauce thickens and is very hot. Serve immediately.

PORK SPARE-RIBS WITH SWEET-SOUR SAUCE

1½ lbs. spare-ribs
1 carrot sliced
1 tablespoon cornflour
1 cup oil
SAUCE:
¼ cup soy sauce
¾ cup honey or sugar

1 onion, sliced
2 teaspoons soy sauce
½ cup water

¾ cup vinegar
1 tablespoon cornflour

Wash the spare-ribs, cut them into two-inch pieces, and put into half a cup of cold water. Boil for about 30 minutes. Pour off what water remains and place the ribs in a bowl and mix with 2 teaspoons of soy sauce, 1 tablespoon of cornflour and a little water.

Heat a frying pan, add the oil and when it is hot fry the spare-ribs until they are brown, stirring frequently. Remove them, drain and place on a warm dish. Reheat the pan and add a tablespoon of the drained oil. When hot fry the carrot and onion for 1 minute. Mix the sauce ingredients and add them to the vegetables. Bring the whole thing to a boil and then add the spare-ribs. When the sauce thickens and is hot, serve immediately.

If you wish, a small cucumber can be substituted for the carrot. Always taste the sweet-sour sauce to make sure it is not too sour. If it is, add a little sugar or honey.

PIG'S FEET AND SWEET-SOUR SAUCE

1 *pair pig's feet*
4 *tablespoons soy sauce*
1 *cup sugar*

1 *ginger root*
3 *tablespoons oil*
1 *cup vinegar*

Wash, clean and scald the pig's feet and then, with a cleaver, cut them into two-inch lengths. Heat a frying pan and add the oil and when it is quite hot add the pig's feet and sauté until browned. Add the soy sauce and continue frying for 1 minute. Then add the sugar and mix well until it melts and blends with the liquid in the pan. Slice the ginger root and add to the pan and finally add the vinegar gradually, stirring all the time. Cover the pan and simmer for about 40 minutes or until the pork is quite tender and the meat will part from the bones easily. Serve immediately.

ROAST PORK

1 *lb. lean pork*
piece ginger, sliced
⅔ *cup soy sauce*
¼ *cup sherry*

4 *spring onions*
1 *onion, sliced*
3 *tablespoons sugar*
½ *teaspoon salt*

Cube the pork not smaller than half an inch and smear it with a mixture of the salt, soy sauce, sherry and sugar. Then add the onion, sliced, the spring onions cut into inch lengths, and the ginger (about the size of a large walnut) sliced thinly. Allow the pork to marinate for an hour. Then place in a baking dish and roast in a moderate oven until it is brown. This should take about 30 minutes. Serve hot.

CANTON ROAST PORK

2 lbs. shoulder pork
1 teaspoon salt
3 teaspoons soy sauce

4 teaspoons sugar
4 teaspoons honey
3 tablespoons chicken stock

Mix together sugar, salt, honey, soy sauce and chicken stock and marinate the pork, cut into four equal pieces, for 45 minutes. Remove from the bowl and place the pork on a rack in a roasting pan with a little water in the pan to prevent smoking. Heat an oven to 350 degrees and roast for at least an hour and 15 minutes longer if the pork is not very tender. Turn it occasionally during the roasting so that all sides get equally cooked. Slice pork and serve immediately.

PORK WITH CHESTNUTS

1½ lbs. pork
1 onion, sliced
1 tablespoon sherry
6 tablespoons soy sauce
2 tablespoons oil

15 chestnuts
1 piece ginger
4 tablespoons brown sugar
¼ teaspoon salt
2 cups water

Shell and blanch the chestnuts and cut the pork, which should be two-third lean and one-third fat, into inch cubes. Heat a frying pan and add the oil. When it is hot put in the onion, the ginger (sliced) and then the pork. Sauté until the pork is golden brown. Then add salt, sugar, sherry and soy sauce and cook for 10 seconds. Add the water and the chestnuts, cut in half, and simmer until all is tender.

PORK WITH BAMBOO SHOOTS

½ lb. lean pork
4 tablespoons rich stock
SAUCE:
2 tablespoons soy sauce
2 tablespoons sherry

3 good-sized bamboo shoots
1 cup oil

1 tablespoon cornflour
½ teaspoon salt

Cut both the pork and the bamboo shoots into thin slices. Heat a frying pan and add 8 tablespoons of oil and when hot fry the bamboo shoot slices for 2 minutes. Remove them and drain. Roll the sliced pork in the sauce mixture until it is well covered. Heat 2 tablespoons of oil in the pan and sauté the pork until it is cooked. Then add the bamboo shoots and the stock. Cook for about 10 seconds and serve immediately.

PORK WITH LILY BUDS

1 cup diced pork meat
¾ cup day lily buds
1 teaspoon salt
2 teaspoons sugar

1 cup sliced mushrooms
1 tablespoon sherry
3 tablespoons oil

The Chinese are very fond of day lily buds, cooked both with meat and fish. Take flower buds that are not more than two inches long; over that size they will be bitter. Soak them in water for twenty minutes and wash well. Dried day lily buds can sometimes be got in Chinese shops and if these are used they should be soaked in water till they swell to normal size. In that event you want ¾ of a cup of them, measured after they have been soaked. Heat a frying pan, add the oil and when it is hot sauté the sliced pork (medium fat) until it is cooked. Then add the sherry, salt and sugar and finally the lily buds and the sliced mushrooms. Cook all together for three minutes, stirring constantly. Serve immediately.

PORK AND GINGER ROOT

½ lb. pork
4 ozs. ginger root
1 teaspoon sugar
2 tablespoons water

1 onion, sliced
3 tablespoons soy sauce
1 teaspoon cornflour
2 tablespoons oil

Slice the pork thinly and smear it with the dry cornflour. Then soak it in the soy sauce for a few minutes. Heat a frying pan and add the oil. Sauté the pork and onion together until the onion is golden brown. Then add the ginger root finely sliced, the sugar and the water. Cook for 2 minutes more and serve hot.

PORK-FILLED MUSHROOMS

½ lb. lean pork finely chopped
3 tablespoons oil
3 teaspoons soy sauce
1 finely chopped spring onion
¼ cup water

12 mushrooms
2 teaspoons salt
2 tablespoons cornflour
2 tablespoons chicken stock

Either chop the pork finely or pass through a mincer and put it in a mixing bowl. Blend it with 1 tablespoon of oil, 1 teaspoon of salt, a dash of pepper, 1 tablespoon of soy sauce, 1 tablespoon of cornflour and the chopped onion. Remove mushroom stalks and discard. Peel and wash the mushroom caps and fill them with the pork mixture.

Put 2 tablespoons of oil in a heavy heated frying pan and add 1 teaspoon of salt and a little pepper. When the oil is hot place the mushroom caps in it and then add the chicken stock. Cover the pan and cook gently for 20 minutes. Remove the mushrooms and place on a hot serving-dish. Mix together 1 tablespoon cornflour, 1 teaspoon soy sauce and the water. Heat and stir until it thickens, pour over the mushrooms and serve hot.

ROAST PORK SPARE-RIBS

3 lbs. spare-ribs
1 teaspoon salt
6 teaspoons soy sauce

4 teaspoons sugar
3 tablespoons honey
1 cup chicken stock

Mix well together the sugar, salt, honey, soy sauce and stock and soak the spare-ribs in it for an hour. Put the spare-ribs on a rack in a roasting pan with a little water below to prevent smoking. Roast in a moderate oven for about an hour and a quarter, turning them over from time to time. Serve hot.

SLICED PORK AND ASPARAGUS

1 lb. lean pork
4 tablespoons oil
1 small onion
½ cup chicken stock
⅓ cup water

fresh asparagus
1 teaspoon salt and little pepper
1 clove garlic
1 tablespoon cornflour

Cut enough asparagus in three-quarter inch slices to make two cups full. Throw into boiling water and cook for four minutes. Heat a frying pan and put in the oil, salt and pepper and add the pork cut into small slices about an eighth of an inch thick. Sauté until brown and then add the chicken stock and the chopped onion and garlic. Cover the pan, turn the flame down to medium and cook for 20 minutes by which time the meat should be tender. Uncover and add the asparagus. Mix the cornflour and water, pour over the meat and asparagus and cook until the sauce thickens, stirring all the time. Serve hot.

LION'S HEAD

1 *lb. lean pork*
6 *water chestnuts*
1 *tablespoon sherry*
2 *teaspoons cornflour*
1½ *cups oil*
2 *cups water*

2 *medium mushrooms*
1 *egg*
4 *tablespoons soy sauce*
2 *tablespoons sugar*
1 *small celery cabbage*
½ *teaspoon salt*

Chop finely or mince the pork and chop the mushrooms and water chestnuts finely, mixing all these ingredients together. Beat the egg and add to the mixture together with the sherry, soy sauce, cornflour, salt and sugar. Mix together well and then form into three large balls. Heat an iron frying pan and add the oil. When hot fry the meat balls until they are brown. Slice the cabbage, add the water and simmer for 20 minutes. Place the cabbage on a serving dish with the meat balls on top and serve hot.

ROAST PORK WITH MUSHROOMS
AND TURNIPS

1 *lb. fresh pork*	2 *white turnips*
½ *cup chicken stock*	4 *mushrooms*
3 *teaspoons sugar*	1 *teaspoon salt*
4 *teaspoons honey*	3 *teaspoons soy sauce*
3 *tablespoons chicken stock*	2 *tablespoons cornflour*
¼ *cup water*	

Put the sugar, salt, honey, soy sauce and 3 tablespoons of stock in a mixing bowl. Cut the pork into eight or ten pieces and soak for not less than half an hour in the mixing bowl. Then place on a rack in a roasting pan with a little water below and roast for not less than an hour in a moderate oven.

Peel the turnips and slice into quarter-inch thick sticks until you have a cupful. Cook in boiling water for 10 minutes. Put half cup chicken stock into a heated frying pan and add one cupful of sliced mushrooms. Cook for 5 minutes over moderate flame, stirring constantly. Remove from fire and add the pork and turnips. Mix together 2 tablespoons of cornflour and ¼ cup water. Add this to the pan and return to the fire and cook until the sauce thickens. Serve hot.

STEWED PORK SPARE-RIBS

1 *lb. spare-ribs*	2 *tablespoons bean curd*
1 *small chopped onion*	1 *clove garlic chopped finely*
2 *tablespoons soy beans*	1 *large white turnip*
1 *tablespoon sugar*	2 *tablespoons oil*
1½ *cups water*	1 *tablespoon soy sauce*

Wash the spare-ribs and cut into pieces not bigger than two inches. Into a hot pan put 2 tablespoons of oil and fry the onion and garlic until they are brown. Add the spare-ribs and fry for 1 minute. Then add the beans, bean curd, soy sauce and sugar and sauté them for 2 or 3 seconds. Add the water and simmer for 15 minutes. Then add the turnips and cook gently until spare-ribs are tender.

STEWED PORK

1 lb. fresh pork	2 spring onions
4 tablespoons sherry	2 tablespoons oil
½ cup soy sauce	1 tablespoon sugar
6 hard boiled eggs	1½ cups water

Cut the pork into pieces about one inch by two and put in a pot with 2 cups of water. Bring to the boil and boil for 2 minutes. Remove the pork. Heat a frying pan and add the oil. When hot put in the onions, cut into inch pieces, add the pork and fry for 1 minute. Then add the sherry, soy sauce, sugar, hard boiled eggs (whole) and 1½ cups of water. Simmer until the pork is tender and serve hot.

STEAMED PORK

1 lb. lean pork	10 water chestnuts
1 onion	3 mushrooms
3 tablespoons soy sauce	2 tablespoons oil
1 teaspoon cornflour	½ teaspoon salt

Chop finely the pork, chestnuts, onion and mushroom and mix them together. Then add the soy sauce, salt, oil and cornflour. Place in a steamer and cook for not less than 20 minutes over fiercely boiling water.

STEAMED PORK AND POTATOES

1 *lb. pork*
1 *clove garlic*
⅓ *cup bean curd*
3 *tablespoons soy sauce*
¼ *teaspoon salt*

3 *potatoes*
small piece of ginger
2 *tablespoons sugar*
2 *tablespoons oil*
1 *chopped onion*

Boil the pork, whole, in 2 cups of water for 3 minutes and then place on one side to cool. Cut the garlic and ginger into very small pieces and put into a frying pan with the heated oil. Cook until the onion is brown and then add the pork and sauté for 1 minute. Add the soy sauce, sugar and salt. When the sugar melts add the bean curd and sauté until it is brown. Remove from the fire and cool. Cut the pork into two-inch pieces and soak in the sauce left in the pan. Slice the potatoes and arrange pork and potatoes alternately and steam for one hour until pork and potatoes are cooked. Serve hot.

BRAISED HAM

2 *lb. slice of ham*
2 *tablespoons sherry*
1 *teaspoon salt*
2 *spring onions*
½ *cup water*

6 *tablespoons soy sauce*
4 *tablespoons sugar, preferably brown*
1 *piece fresh ginger*
4 *tablespoons oil*

Boil the ham for 5 minutes. Remove and drain. Then smear it with the soy sauce, sherry and salt. Heat a frying pan, add the oil and stir in the sugar to make a syrup. Cut the green parts of the onions into inch pieces and add to the syrup together with the ginger, sliced, and the ham. Brown the ham well. Then add the sauce in which the ham was marinated and the water. Simmer for 5 seconds, place in a large bowl and steam for an hour by which time the ham should be very tender. Place the ham on a serving dish, cut into thin slices, pour over it what sauce remains and serve hot.

PORK WITH CELERY

½ lb. lean fresh pork
6 tablespoons oil
1 teaspoon sherry
½ teaspoon salt
MIX TOGETHER
1 teaspoon sherry
1 tablespoon cornflour

2 heads celery
2 tablespoons soy sauce
¼ cup stock

1 tablespoon soy sauce

Slice the pork thinly and smear thoroughly with the mixture. Heat a frying pan and add 4 tablespoons of oil and sauté the pork for 5 seconds. Place the pork on one side, reheat the pan and in 2 tablespoons of oil sauté for 5 seconds the celery sliced diagonally into inch lengths. Then to the celery add soy sauce, salt, sherry and stock. Lastly put the sliced pork in and sauté for a few minutes until done. Serve hot.

PORK AND CUCUMBER

¼ lb. fresh pork
2 tablespoons oil
MIX TOGETHER:
¼ teaspoon cornflour
1 tablespoon soy sauce

2 small cucumbers
4 tablespoons water

½ teaspoon salt

Slice the pork thinly and smear with the cornflour, soy sauce and salt mixture. Cut the cucumbers into quarters lengthwise and then slice each quarter into half-inch pieces diagonally. Heat a frying pan, add the oil and when hot sauté the pork. Add the water and simmer for a minute. Then add the cucumbers and when they are heated through serve hot.

SZECHUEN TWICE-COOKED PORK

2 lbs. pork rib roast	1 spring onion
3 cups water	1 tablespoon oil
1 tablespoon soy sauce	½ clove garlic
4 thin slices ginger	1 teaspoon sugar

dash of cayenne pepper or ½ teaspoon tabasco sauce

Put the pork in saucepan with the water, bring to the boil and simmer for 1 hour. Remove from water and cool. Remove the bones. Slice the meat a quarter of an inch thick against the grain and then cut each slice in two. Put 1 tablespoon of oil in a hot pan and add the bruised garlic and the onion cut into half-inch sections. Cook for a few seconds and then add the pork slices, the soy sauce, ginger and either the cayenne pepper or tabasco sauce and cook for 5 minutes, turning and stirring the whole time. Serve hot.

DICED PORK WITH ALMONDS

1 lb. lean pork	¼ cup almonds, blanched
2 cups carrots, diced	1 cup of shelled peas
2 cups diced celery	½ cup chicken broth
4 tablespoons oil	1 teaspoon salt
2 tablespoons cornflour	1 tablespoon soy sauce
⅛ cup water	

Chop the almonds and cook in a little oil until golden brown, stirring them constantly so they don't burn. Drain and put aside. Cook the carrots and peas in boiling water for 5 minutes. In a hot frying pan put 4 tablespoons of oil, 1 teaspoon of salt and the pork cut into half-inch cubes. Cook over moderate flame until golden brown. Then add the celery and the chicken broth together with the cooked carrots and peas. Cover the pan and cook over a low flame for 5 minutes. Mix the cornflour, soy sauce and ⅓ cup of water and add to the cooked ingredients. Stir the whole mixture constantly until the sauce thickens. Finally stir in the almonds and when they are heated through serve the dish very hot.

PORK STUFFED PEPPERS

1 *lb. lean pork*
3 *tablespoons oil*
2 *tablespoons soy sauce*
1 *spring onion*
¼ *cup water*

4 *green sweet peppers*
2 *teaspoon salt*
2 *tablespoons cornflour*
½ *cup chicken stock*

Chop the meat or put through a mincer and place in a mixing bowl with 1 tablespoon of oil, 1 teaspoon of salt, 1 tablespoon of soy sauce, dash of pepper, 1 tablespoon of cornflour. Mix thoroughly. Chop the onion finely and mix it in.

Remove stalk end of peppers and scoop out the seeds. Wash well and fill with the pork mixture. Put 2 tablespoons of oil in a hot frying pan and add 1 teaspoon of salt and dash of pepper. When the oil is hot place the filled peppers in and add the chicken stock. Cover the pan, turn the flame low and gently cook for an hour. Place the peppers in a warm serving dish. Add to the liquid in the pan 1 tablespoon of cornflour, 1 tablespoon of soy sauce and the water. Cook this sauce for a few minutes, stirring constantly, pour it over the peppers and serve.

HAM WITH HONEY

1 *lb. ham.*   ½ *cup honey*
½ *cup sherry*   *cornflour*

The ham must be well cured, of the York or Virginia type.
Place it whole in a frying pan over a low flame with the honey
and sherry and cook gently, keeping flame low, for half an
hour. Turn it constantly so that it does not burn or even
brown and baste it frequently with the sauce.

Remove the ham, cut into small slices. Arrange these on a
serving dish. Add enough cornflour to thicken the sauce and
pour it over the ham. Serve immediately.

If you feel very ambitious the more correct method is to
take a whole ham. Cook it, preferably by baking, then add
enough sherry and honey in equal quantities to make ample
basting sauce. Baste continually for half an hour.

Slice in small pieces enough ham for the number of guests
present and place them on a serving dish. Take a generous
quantity of the basting sauce, thicken it with cornflour and
pour over the ham. Serve immediately.

PORK WITH EGGS AND MUSHROOMS

½ *lb. pork*   4 *eggs, beaten*
10 *mushrooms*   4 *tablespoons oil*
3 *tablespoons water*
SAUCE:
3 *tablespoons soy sauce*   1 *teaspoon cornflour*
1 *tablespoon sherry*   ½ *teaspoon salt*

Mix together the sauce ingredients, slice the pork thinly and
soak in the mixture for a few minutes. Heat a frying pan, add
the oil and when hot scramble the eggs. Remove them and
place on one side. Reheat the pan, add the rest of the oil and

sauté the pork and the mushrooms, sliced coarsely, for 1 minute. Then add the eggs and cook for about a minute.

Be sure to slice the pork very finely, or it will not cook in the time.

HAM AND EGG OMELETTE

½ lb. ham
½ cup celery
½ cup bamboo shoots
2 teaspoons salt
dash pepper
1 teaspoon sugar

5 eggs, beaten
½ cup onions, chopped
½ cup water chestnuts
2 teaspoons soy sauce
1 tablespoon flour
½ cup oil

Heat a frying pan and add 3 tablespoons of oil. When it is hot sauté the vegetables for 1 minute. The celery should be diced and the bamboo shoots and water chestnuts sliced. Then add to the pan the soy sauce, salt, sugar and pepper. Cook for a couple of seconds and place the vegetables on a dish to cool.

Sprinkle the flour into the mixture, stirring so that it goes in smoothly. Then combine the mixture with the beaten eggs. Finally add the ham, chopped or shredded, and mix all ingredients well.

Reheat the pan, add 2 tablespoons of oil and when it is hot drop in two tablespoons of the mixture and brown lightly on both sides. Continue until all the mixture is cooked, adding oil to the pan as required.

STEAMED LEG OF PORK

1 *small leg of pork*	1 *lb. spinach*
2 *cloves garlic*	1 *piece red bean curd*
1 *tablespoon aniseed*	2 *tablespoons thick soy sauce*
6 *tablespoons soy sauce*	3 *tablespoons sugar*
1 *teaspoon salt*	3 *teaspoons sherry*
2 *tablespoons cornflour*	3 *cups water*
4 *tablespoons oil*	

The leg should be quite small. Wash it and prick the skin all over, fairly deeply, with a pointed knife. Smear it with 2 tablespoons of soy sauce. Put it in two cups of water and boil for 30 minutes. Remove the leg and place in a bowl of cold water.

Heat a large frying pan, add the oil and when it is hot add the garlic, crushed, and fry until it is brown. Then add the cooled pork and brown it on all sides. Add the salt, the bean curd, the rest of the soy sauce and 2 tablespoons sugar. Continue cooking for one minute. Then add the cornflour mixed in 1 cup of water. Cook for a second more and then remove the pork and put in a deep bowl. Pour all the liquid from the pan over the pork, adding 1 tablespoon of sugar, the sherry and the thick soy sauce. Finally put the aniseed on top of the pork, cover and steam for 1 hour or longer if it is not then tender.

Just before the pork is done wash the spinach thoroughly, cut it into two-inch lengths and put in boiling water. Cook for 5 minutes, remove it, drain and place on a large platter.

Remove the aniseed from the pork and place the pork on the bed of spinach. Add 2 teaspoons of cornflour to the sauce in the bowl to thicken it. Let it boil for a second or two and then pour over the pork and spinach. Serve immediately.

The pork should be so tender that the meat can be taken from the bones with chopsticks.

STEAMED PORK WITH CARROTS AND TURNIPS

1 lb. pork
4 tablespoons diced white turnips
1 teaspoon salt
1 teaspoon cornflour

4 tablespoons diced carrots
2 spring onions
dash pepper
1 teaspoon soy sauce
2 tablespoons oil

Chop the pork finely or put through a mincer and put it in a mixing bowl. Sprinkle over it 1 teaspoon of salt, a dash of pepper, 1 teaspoon of cornflour, 1 teaspoon of soy sauce and 1 tablespoon of oil. Blend thoroughly and then add the vegetables, chopping the onions finely. If the mixture does not blend well add a little more oil.

Place the mixture in a shallow dish or casserole and put this in a deep cooking pan on a rack. In the bottom of the pan put half an inch of water. Cover the pan tightly and steam the pork over a low flame for an hour and a quarter. Serve immediately.

STEAMED PORK WITH VEGETABLES

1 cup chopped pork
1 cup chopped bamboo shoots
½ teaspoon salt
1 teaspoon sugar
2 tablespoons oil

1 cup diced water chestnuts
4 tablespoons chopped pickled cucumber
3 tablespoons soy sauce
1 tablespoon sherry

Place the chopped pork in a mixture of the salt, soy sauce, sugar, oil and sherry. Allow to marinate for a few minutes. Then add the water chestnuts, bamboo shoots and cucumber. Mix together, place in a bowl and steam for 40 minutes. Serve immediately.

PORK WITH GREEN PEPPER AND NOODLES

1 *lb. pork*	1 *small onion, chopped*
½ *clove garlic*	2 *green peppers*
1 *cup diced celery*	1 *cup chicken stock*
2 *tablespoons oil*	1 *teaspoon salt*
dash pepper	
SAUCE:	
2 *tablespoons cornflour*	*little water*
2 *teaspoons soy sauce*	

Heat a frying pan and add the oil, salt and dash of pepper When hot add the pork cut into half-inch cubes, the onion and the garlic, chopped. Sauté over a moderate flame until the pork is nicely browned, stirring constantly, and then add the stock. Cover and simmer over low flame for ten minutes. Uncover and add the sweet peppers cut into pieces about half an inch square and the diced celery. Cover again and continue cooking over low flame for 5 minutes.

Have some cooked noodles ready and add them to the pork and vegetables, mixing all the ingredients. Then add the sauce mixture and continue cooking, stirring all the time, until the sauce thickens and the noodles are hot. Serve immediately.

PORK STUFFED LOTUS ROOT

3 *sections lotus root*	2 *eggs, beaten*
2 *tablespoons cornflour*	*oil for deep frying*
	2 *tablespoons flour*
STUFFING:	
4 *ozs. minced pork*	1 *teaspoon chopped ginger*
½ *cup tightly packed spinach*	1 *tablespoon soy sauce*
1 *small onion, finely chopped*	1 *teaspoon salt*

Cook the spinach for 5 minutes in boiling water, drain, then chop finely and leave on one side. Heat a frying pan and add 2 tablespoons of oil. When hot sauté the minced pork and the finely chopped onion for 2 minutes. Remove from the pan and mix the pork, onion, ginger, soy sauce and salt together.

Cut the lotus root into slices a quarter of an inch thick. Then with a sharp knife slice each piece down the middle for three-quarters of the way. Open these and stuff with the pork and spinach mixture and press the edges of the lotus root slices together.

Make a batter of the beaten eggs, flour and cornflour and dip in the stuffed lotus root slices. Allow to dry. If they are not completely sealed repeat the process. Put oil in a deep frying pan and bring to about 375 degrees. Place the stuffed slices in the wire basket a few at a time and lower into the hot oil, frying until they are a golden brown. Serve hot.

STEAMED PORK AND EGGS

½ lb. cooked pork
10 water chestnuts
1 spring onion
½ teaspoon salt

4 eggs
2 tablespoons oil
2 teaspoons soy sauce
½ cup cold water

Chop the pork finely. Beat the eggs. Chop the water chestnuts and the onion finely. Heat a skillet and add the oil. When hot sauté the pork and water chestnuts for 1 minute. Add the soy sauce and salt and cook for 5 seconds. Drain the pork and chestnuts and place in a bowl. Add the water and then stir in the beaten eggs. Cover the dish and place over a saucepan of boiling water. Steam for 20 minutes when the eggs should be firm. Serve immediately.

HAM WITH SPINACH

1 *lb. cooked ham*
3 *tablespoons chicken stock*
¼ *clove garlic*
salt to taste

1 *lb. spinach*
2 *tablespoons chopped onion*
2 *tablespoons oil*

SAUCE:
2 *tablespoons cornflour*
1 *teaspoon soy sauce*

½ *teaspoon sugar*
¼ *cup water*

Cut the ham into half-inch cubes. Heat a frying pan and add oil, garlic and the chopped onion. Fry for 5 seconds and then add the ham. Cook, constantly stirring, until the ham is slightly browned.

Wash the spinach well and tear the leaves from the stems, discarding the latter. Add the stock and the spinach to the pan. Cover it and cook over a moderate flame for 5 minutes, turning the spinach twice during the process.

Add the sauce mixture to the pan and cook until the sauce thickens. Serve very hot immediately.

STEWED PORK WITH GINGER

1½ *lbs. fresh pork*   *fresh ginger*
2 *tablespoons sherry*   ¼ *cup soy sauce*
1 *teaspoon salt*   1 *teaspoon sugar*
½ *cup water*

For this use loin of pork, leg or shoulder. Cut the meat into
one-inch cubes and put with the water in an iron frying pan.
When the water comes to the boil add the sherry, salt, soy
sauce and a piece of ginger (about the size of a large walnut)
sliced thinly. Cover the pan and turn the flame down and let
the dish simmer gently for an hour. Add the sugar, cover again
and continue cooking for about 20 minutes. Be sure the meat
is done but on no account overcook. Serve hot.

* * *

The above dish can be varied in many ways with the addition
of vegetables, either one vegetable or two or three. Whatever
vegetables you use cut them in pieces roughly the size of the
meat cubes and add them to the dish with the sugar. Cubed
turnips, carrots, parsnips, yellow turnips, celery, cucumber
can all be used.

PORK WITH GREEN PEAS

1 *cup shelled peas*	½ *lb. pork*
5 *mushrooms*	½ *cup stock*
1 *tablespoon sherry*	1 *teaspoon salt*
1 *tablespoon cornflour*	1 *tablespoon oil*

Cook the peas in boiling salted water for 4 minutes, drain and reserve. Cut the pork into thin slices. Heat a frying pan and add the oil. When hot fry the pork for 10 seconds. Add the salt, sherry and 2 tablespoons of the stock and continue cooking for a few seconds. Then add the sliced mushrooms, the peas and ¼ cup of stock in which the cornflour has been mixed. Continue cooking over a brisk flame for 2 minutes and serve hot.

PORK WITH SHRIMPS

1 *lb. pork*	1 *clove garlic*
1 *medium onion*	½ *cup cooked shrimps*
2 *tablespoons soy sauce*	1 *teaspoon sugar*
2 *tablespoons oil*	1 *cup chicken stock*
1 *teaspoon salt*	

The pork should be at least one third fat. Cut it into inch cubes. Heat a frying pan and add the oil. When hot add the garlic, chopped, and the onion, sliced, and fry until they are brown. Then add the pork and continue frying until it is nicely browned. Then add the soy sauce, the sugar, salt and the shrimps chopped up finely. Continue cooking for a few seconds. Add the stock and simmer until the pork is tender. Serve immediately.

STEWED PORK WITH BEAN CURD

1 *lb. pork*	1 *onion*
1 *clove garlic*	*fresh ginger size of walnut*
4 *tablespoons soy sauce*	1 *tablespoon sugar*
½ *teaspoon salt*	½ *cup bean curd*
3 *tablespoons oil*	1½ *cup chicken stock*

Put the pork into two cups of cold water, bring to the boil and cook for 4 minutes. Remove and leave to cool. Heat a frying pan, add the oil and when hot add the garlic, chopped, and the onion, sliced, and fry until golden brown. Then add the pork and fry it on each side for a minute. Add the bean curd and fry for 1 minute more. Add the soy sauce, salt and sugar and lastly the chicken stock. Cover and allow to simmer until the pork is sufficiently tender to be pulled apart with chopsticks, which should be about half an hour.

PORK OMELETTE

Proceed exactly as for Beef Omelette (page 127), but using minced fresh pork instead of beef.

¶ BEEF

SLICED BEEF WITH VEGETABLES

1 *cup finely sliced beef*
1 *cup diced celery*
3 *tablespoons oil*
dash pepper
1 *tablespoon cornflour*

1 *cup bean sprouts*
1 *diced carrot*
1 *teaspoon salt*
2 *tablespoons soy sauce*
2 *teaspoons of any meat sauce such as Worcestershire*

Boil the carrots and bean sprouts for one minute and then drain. Mix together the soy sauce, salt, pepper, cornflour and meat sauce and let the sliced beef soak in it for a couple of minutes. Put 2 tablespoons oil into a hot frying pan and fry the carrot, bean sprouts and celery for 1 minute and then place them on one side. In the rest of the oil sauté the beef, also for 1 minute, turning frequently. Add the vegetables to the beef and cook together for about a minute, still stirring. Finally add 2 tablespoons of water, cook for 5 seconds more and serve hot.

BEEF WITH MUSHROOMS

¾ *lb. lean beef*
½ *cup beef stock*
2 *tablespoons oil*
sliver of garlic
1 *tablespoon soy sauce*

¾ *lb. mushrooms*
1 *small onion*
1 *teaspoon salt and dash pepper*
2 *tablespoons cornflour*

Into a hot frying pan put 2 tablespoons oil and the salt and pepper and add the beef cut into small slices about an eighth of an inch thick. Sauté over a fairly hot flame until the meat browns, stirring it constantly. Then add the beef stock and the mushrooms, sliced. Cover the pan and cook fairly briskly for 5 minutes. Blend together the cornflour, soy sauce and a quarter of a cup of water. Add this to the pan and cook until the sauce thickens, stirring constantly. Serve hot.

BEEF WITH GREEN PEPPERS

¾ *lb. lean beef*
1 *clove garlic*
1 *teaspoon salt*
1 *spring onion*
1 *cup beef stock*
1 *tablespoon soy sauce*

3 *green peppers*
3 *tablespoons oil*
dash of pepper
1 *cup diced celery*
2 *teaspoons cornflour*

Cut the beef as in the previous recipe and add to 3 tablespoons of oil in a very hot frying pan. Add salt and pepper and cook, stirring constantly, until the beef is browned. Then add the onion, chopped into half-inch pieces, the garlic (chopped) and the peppers (sliced). Then add the celery and the beef stock and cook gently for 10 minutes under a cover. Mix the cornflour and soy sauce with ¼ cup of water and add this to the pan. Cook until the sauce thickens, stirring all the time, and serve hot.

BEEF WITH STRING BEANS

½ lb. good lean beef
MIX TOGETHER
2 tablespoons oil
1 tablespoon sherry
2 tablespoons soy sauce

½ lb. string beans

1 tablespoon cornflour
1 teaspoon sugar
½ teaspoon salt and pepper

Slice the beef into pieces about one inch by two and soak in the mixture for 2 or 3 minutes. Heat a frying pan, add a tablespoon of oil and cook the beef for 5 seconds. Remove the beef. In the meantime have the beans sliced lengthwise and cook them for 3 minutes in a cup of water and then drain them. Reheat the pan and add 1 tablespoon of oil. When hot sauté the beans for 5 seconds, add the beef and also 2 or 3 tablespoons of the water the beans were boiled in. Simmer for 3 minutes. and serve.

BEEF WITH CABBAGE

½ lb. lean beef
¼ cup beef stock
½ teaspoon salt
1 small onion
MIX WELL TOGETHER:
2 tablespoons soy sauce
1 teaspoon sugar
2 teaspoons sherry

4 cups sliced cabbage
3 tablespoons oil
dash of pepper

2 teaspoons cornflour
½ teaspoon salt

Heat a frying pan and add 1 tablespoon of oil and the stock. When hot, add the cabbage and cook for 1 minute and then remove to a dish. Reheat the pan and sauté the sliced onion for 5 seconds in 1 tablespoon of oil. Add the finely sliced beef and sauté for 5 seconds more. Add the cabbage, fry all together for 2 minutes, stirring constantly, and serve hot.

BEEF WITH ONIONS

½ lb. good lean beef
3 tablespoons oil
1 tablespoon soy sauce
½ teaspoon salt

MIX TOGETHER:
2 teaspoons cornflour
2 teaspoons soy sauce

3 large onions
1 tablespoon sherry
½ teaspoon sugar
dash pepper

saltspoon salt
1 teaspoon sherry

Slice the beef thinly and soak it in the mixture. Slice the onion finely. Heat a frying pan and add half the oil. When hot sauté the beef for a minute. Remove the beef, add the rest of the oil to the pan and sauté the onions until they begin to brown. Add salt, soy sauce, sugar and sherry to the pan and then the beef. Cook together for 1 minute and serve hot.

BEEF WITH CAULIFLOWER AND PEAS

¾ lb. lean beef
1 small head cauliflower
1 lb. shelled peas
2 tablespoons oil

MIX TOGETHER:
2 tablespoons cornflour
2 teaspoons soy sauce

1 small onion
sliver of garlic
1 cup beef stock
1 teaspoon salt

¼ cup water

Slice the beef thinly and also the onion. Put them, with the garlic, into a hot frying pan with 2 tablespoons of oil and the salt. Cook over a moderate flame until the meat browns. Then add the beef stock and the cauliflower pulled apart into 'flowerets', and the peas. Cover the pan, turn the flame as low as possible and cook for about 10 minutes. Then add the mixture of cornflour, soy sauce and water and cook until the sauce thickens, not more than 5 minutes. Serve hot immediately.

BEEF WITH CUCUMBERS

¾ *lb. lean beef*
½ *cup stock (chicken or beef)*
2 *teaspoons salt*
dash pepper

3 *small cucumbers*
1 *spring onion*
2 *teaspoons cornflour*
4 *tablespoons oil*

Slice the beef thinly and place in a mixing bowl with 2 teaspoons of cornflour, 1 teaspoon salt and 2 tablespoons of oil and leave for few minutes. Heat a frying pan and add 2 tablespoons of oil, 1 teaspoon of salt and dash of pepper. Sauté the meat over a moderate flame until it browns. Cut the cucumbers in quarters, lengthwise, and scoop out the seeds. Slice the pieces diagonally and add to the meat together with the stock. Cover the pan and cook gently for 5 minutes or until the cucumber is tender. Chop the onion finely and add to the pan. Cook for 5 seconds more and serve hot.

BEEF WITH RADISHES

½ *lb. lean beef*
3 *tablespoons oil*
1 *teaspoon cornflour*
SWEET-SOUR SAUCE:
⅓ *cup vinegar*
⅓ *cup sugar*

10 *radishes*
2 *tablespoons soy sauce*

1 *tablespoon cornflour*

Slice the beef thinly and smear it with a mixture of 2 tablespoons of soy sauce and 1 teaspoon of cornflour. Heat a frying pan and add 2 tablespoons of oil. When hot pour into it the sweet-sour sauce mixture and stir. Put the beef in and cook until it ceases to be pink. Lastly add the radishes, sliced, and cook for not longer than a second so that they remain crisp. Serve immediately.

BEEF WITH ASPARAGUS

¾ lb. lean beef   asparagus
¼ cup beef stock   small onion
3 tablespoons oil   1 teaspoon salt
1 tablespoon cornflour   ⅛ cup water

Cut fresh asparagus diagonally, enough to fill two cups, and cook in boiling water for 5 minutes. Slice the beef thinly. Heat a frying pan and add 3 tablespoons of oil and 1 teaspoon of salt. When hot add the beef and brown it quickly, stirring constantly. Dice the onion and add to the beef. Cover and cook gently for 15 minutes. Then add the asparagus and with it the cornflour mixed with the water. Cook gently and stir constantly until the sauce thickens and then serve immediately, very hot.

SWEET AND SOUR MEAT BALLS

1 lb. minced beef
1 egg
1½ teaspoons salt
⅓ cup chicken stock

SWEET-SOUR SAUCE:
3 teaspoons cornflour
2 teaspoons soy sauce
½ cup vinegar

3 green peppers
2 tablespoons flour
½ cup oil
3 slices tinned pineapple

½ cup sugar
½ cup chicken broth

Cut each pepper into six or eight pieces and boil for 5 minutes. Form the minced beef into small meat balls and dip them in a batter made of the egg, 2 tablespoons of flour, ½ teaspoon of salt and a dash of pepper. Heat a frying pan and add to it half a cup of oil and 1 teaspoon of salt. When hot put in the meat balls and fry over moderate flame until they are golden brown one side. This should be about 5 minutes. Turn and brown the other side. Place the meat balls on one side and retain in the pan 1 tablespoon of oil to which add ⅓ cup of chicken stock and the pineapple rings each cut into eight pieces. Cook over a low flame for 8 minutes. Blend the ingredients of the sweet-sour sauce and add to the frying pan. Stir constantly until the sauce thickens, which should be about 5 minutes. Then pour contents of the pan over the meat balls and serve immediately.

BROILED BEEF

1½ lbs. beef, preferably tender-   3 tablespoons soy sauce
   loin (fillet)   2 teaspoons sugar
1 teaspoon salt   1 clove garlic

Cut the beef against the grain into slices half an inch or more
thick. Crush the garlic and mix it with the soy sauce, the sugar
and the salt. Soak the beef in this mixture for at least 15
minutes. In any event don't remove until immediately before
cooking. Grill the beef under (or over) a fierce flame for 2
minutes on each side and serve at once.

BEEF HEART WITH GINGER

1 beef or veal heart   2 spring onions
ginger root   2 tablespoons soy sauce
2 tablespoons sherry   2 tablespoons oil
1 tablespoon cornflour   1 teaspoon sugar
1 teaspoon salt

Clean the heart of all fat and blood vessels. Cut it vertically in
four and then cut horizontal slices about a quarter of an inch
thick. Cut the onions finely and add to the meat together with
the soy sauce, sherry, cornflour, salt, sugar, three or four thin
slices of ginger and about 2 tablespoons of water. Leave the
meat to marinate for a few minutes.

Heat a frying pan, add the oil and when hot put in the meat
and cook over moderate flame for 4 minutes, stirring constantly, by which time the meat should be tender. If not cook
1 more minute and serve immediately.

FRIED BEEF KIDNEY

1 lb. slices beef kidney
2 tablespoons sherry
1 tablespoon cornflour
2 tablespoons oil

1 small onion
2 tablespoons soy sauce
½ teaspoon salt

Slice the kidneys down to the core and discard that. Soak the slices in water for half an hour and then wash thoroughly. Mix together the sherry, soy sauce, cornflour (mixed with a little water), the salt and the onion chopped very finely. Mix the kidney slices with this sauce and leave for a few minutes.

Heat a frying pan, add the oil and when it is hot sauté the kidney for 3 or 4 minutes, stirring constantly. Serve immediately.

BEEF WITH LOTUS ROOT

½ lb. lean beef, sliced
2 tablespoons soy sauce
¼ teaspoon sugar
3 tablespoons water

2 cups sliced lotus root
1 teaspoon salt
4 tablespoons oil

Heat a frying pan and add 3 tablespoons of oil. When it is hot sauté the sliced lotus root for 3 minutes. Remove and reserve in a warm place. Reheat the pan and add 1 tablespoon of oil to that already there and sauté the beef slices after mixing them with the soy sauce, salt and sugar. Fry the beef briskly for 1 minute then return the sliced lotus root to the pan and cook for 3 minutes more, stirring constantly. See that the lotus root is cut quite thinly. Serve immediately.

STEAMED MINCED BEEF

1½ cups minced beef   ½ cup chopped parsnip
1 teaspoon chopped ginger   3 tablespoons soy sauce
1 tablespoon sherry   1 teaspoon sugar
2 tablespoons oil

With a fork mix the soy sauce, sherry, sugar and oil into the minced beef. When well blended add the parsnip, finely chopped, and the ginger and mix well. Place in a dish over boiling water and steam for 25 minutes. Serve immediately.

MINCED BEEF WITH NOODLES

½ lb. minced beef   3 ozs. dry noodles
4 tablespoons chopped onion   ½ clove garlic
3 medium tomatoes   ¾ cup beef stock
½ cup celery   1 green pepper
2 tablespoons oil   1 teaspoon salt and dash pepper
SAUCE:
2 teaspoons cornflour   3 tablespoons water
2 teaspoons soy sauce

Cook the noodles in boiling salted water until tender then drain and set aside.

Heat a frying pan and add the oil. When it is hot add salt, pepper, minced beef, the onion, the crushed garlic and tomatoes (cubed). Simmer for five minutes, stirring constantly. Then add the beef stock, the diced celery and the finely chopped peppers. Cover the pan and simmer for 5 minutes more.

Mix the sauce ingredients and add to the pan. Continue cooking over a moderate flame for 5 minutes more by which time the sauce should be thickened. Pour contents of pan over the noodles and serve immediately.

BEEF WITH SPINACH AND POTATOES

½ lb. fairly lean beef
¼ clove garlic, chopped
½ cup beef stock
3 tablespoons oil
SAUCE:
1 tablespoon cornflour
3 tablespoons water

1 small onion, chopped
2 cups cubed potatoes, raw
4 ozs. spinach
1 teaspoon salt and dash pepper

2 teaspoons soy sauce

Slice the beef diagonally across the grain in slices an eighth of an inch thick. Cut the potatoes into half-inch cubes and run a knife across the spinach every two inches.

Heat a frying pan and add the oil. When hot add salt and pepper and the sliced beef. Brown this quickly over a high flame, stirring constantly. Then add the garlic, onion, raw potatoes and beef stock. Turn the flame down, cover the pan and simmer until the potatoes are cooked, about 10 minutes. Wash the spinach well and add to the pan. Cover the pan again and simmer for 5 minutes more. Blend the sauce ingredients together and add to the pan and cook a little longer, stirring constantly, until the sauce thickens. Serve immediately.

BEEF WITH OYSTER SAUCE

½ lb. beef flank
2 teaspoons cornflour
2 tablespoons oil
1 cup sliced mushrooms
½ cup beef stock

1 cup rice
2 teaspoons soy sauce
1 teaspoon salt and dash pepper
1 spring onion

Cook the rice, drain and reserve. Slice the beef thinly and put in a mixing bowl with the cornflour, soy sauce, salt and pepper, and finally the mushrooms. Leave to soak a few minutes. Heat a frying pan, add the oil and when hot sauté the beef, mushrooms and the chopped onion until the beef is cooked, about 5 minutes. Add the stock and simmer, covered, for 2 minutes. Add two tablespoons oyster sauce, continuing cooking for few seconds. Arrange the warm rice on a dish and pour over it contents of pan. Serve immediately.

OYSTER SAUCE

1 *doz. raw oysters*   1 *cup oyster liquid*
3 *tablespoons soy sauce*

Chop the oysters finely and put in a saucepan with the oyster liquid. Bring this to the boil, cover and simmer gently for about twenty minutes. Remove and strain through a fine sieve and add to it the soy sauce. Reserve for use as a seasoning ingredient or as a sauce.

STEAMED BEEF

1 *lb. lean beef*   2 *spring onions*
1 *teaspoon cornflour*   1 *teaspoon salt and dash pepper*
2 *teaspoons soy sauce*   1 *tablespoon oil*
2 *tablespoons sherry*   1 *teaspoon vinegar*

Slice the beef into slivers an eighth of an inch thick. Place them in the bottom of a bowl. Blend well together the cornflour, salt, pepper, soy sauce, oil, sherry and vinegar. Pour this over the beef. Chop the onions very finely and sprinkle on top.

Cover tightly, place over a saucepan of boiling water and steam for 45 minutes or until the beef is quite tender. Serve immediately.

MINCED BEEF WITH STRING BEANS

1 *lb. minced beef*
1 *small onion, chopped*
1 *cup beef stock*
4 *tablespoons oil*
SAUCE:
3 *teaspoons cornflour*

1 *lb. string beans*
¼ *clove garlic*
3 *eggs*
1 *teaspoon salt*

¼ *cup water*

Slice the beans and boil for 5 minutes. Drain and place on one side. Heat a frying pan and add the oil and salt. When hot add the beef, the chopped onion and the garlic. Cook, stirring constantly, until the beef is cooked through. Then add beans and beef stock, cover the pan and simmer for four minutes. Beat the eggs and pour over the beef and vegetables, stirring rapidly as it goes in. Cook over a low flame until the eggs begin to thicken. Blend the cornflour and water together, add to the pan and cook, stirring constantly, until the sauce thickens. Serve immediately.

BEEF WITH CAULIFLOWER

1 *cauliflower*	½ *cup sliced beef*
4 *tablespoons oil*	1 *teaspoon salt*
1 *tablespoon soy sauce*	

SAUCE:

2 *teaspoons cornflour*	½ *teaspoon salt*
2 *tablespoons soy sauce*	4 *tablespoons water*

Break enough flowerets off the cauliflower to fill two cups. Blend the sauce ingredients together and soak the beef in it. Heat a frying pan and add the oil. When hot sauté the cauliflower for 5 seconds. Then add soy sauce and salt, fry 1 second more and remove contents of the pan.

Reheat the pan, add 2 tablespoons of oil and when hot fry the beef for 2 minutes. Return the cauliflower to the pan and add ¼ cup of cold water. Bring to the boil and simmer for 3 minutes. Serve immediately.

BEEF WITH BAMBOO SHOOTS AND PEAPODS

1 *lb. lean beef*	1 *large bamboo shoot*
12 *peapods*	*fresh ginger*
2 *tablespoons sherry*	3 *tablespoons soy sauce*
1 *teaspoon salt*	1 *teaspoon sugar*
½ *cup water*	

Slice the beef so that the pieces are about an eighth of an inch thick and two inches square. Put in a frying pan with the water and when the water boils add the sherry, soy sauce, salt and about three thin slices of ginger root. Cover and cook very gently for about 45 minutes. Cut the bamboo shoot so that it is like rather small French fried potatoes about two inches long and add them to the pan together with the whole peapods and the sugar. Cover again and cook for 10 minutes. Serve immediately.

BEEF WITH CABBAGE

1 *small cabbage*	½ *lb. beef, lean*
2 *tablespoons oil*	
SAUCE:	
1 *teaspoon salt*	1 *tablespoon sherry*
1 *tablespoon sugar*	1 *teaspoon chopped fresh ginger*
3 *tablespoons soy sauce*	

Select a tight head of cabbage, quarter it and then cut each quarter in half. Cook it in boiling salted water for 2 minutes, remove and drain.

Slice the beef thinly and soak it for 5 minutes in the sauce mixture. Heat a pan, add the oil and when hot fry the beef slices for 1 minute. Then add the cabbage and continue cooking for 3 minutes, turning frequently. Serve hot immediately.

BEEF WITH MUSTARD GREENS

½ *lb. lean beef*	*mustard greens*
2 *tablespoons oil*	*fresh ginger*
¼ *cup water or stock*	
SAUCE:	
1 *tablespoon sherry*	½ *teaspoon salt*
2 *teaspoons cornflour*	2 *teaspoons sugar*
1 *tablespoon soy sauce*	

Slice the beef thinly and soak it a few minutes in the sauce mixture. Heat a frying pan, add the oil and when hot sauté the beef for ten seconds over a brisk flame. Slice the ginger finely and add to the pan together with enough mustard greens to make two tightly packed cups when cut into two-inch lengths. Fry for 10 seconds then add the water or stock and simmer for 5 minutes. This recipe assumes the beef is tenderloin (fillet). If a tougher cut is used fry it somewhat longer. Serve hot.

BEEF OMELETTE

6 *eggs*	¾ *lb. lean minced beef*
1 *onion*	1 *tablespoon soy sauce*
½ *teaspoon sugar*	⅓ *cup oil*
SAUCE MIXTURE:	
1 *teaspoon cornflour*	1 *tablespoon sherry*
½ *teaspoon salt*	

Beat the eggs lightly and leave on one side. Mix the minced (or ground) beef thoroughly with the sauce mixture. Slice the onion finely.

Put half the oil in a hot frying pan and when the oil is hot put in the onion and fry to a light brown. Then add the meat mixture, soy sauce and sugar. Continue cooking until the meat browns, then remove it and set aside.

Pour off the oil and then return a teaspoonful to the pan. Put in the pan about a tablespoon of the beaten eggs and when it begins to set place on it a teaspoon of the meat mixture and fold half the tiny omelette over on top of it. Fry until done, turning once. Continue until egg and meat mixture are used up. There should be enough for about 15 individual omelettes. Serve hot immediately. Pork omelettes can be made in the same way.

E

¶ LAMB

LAMB WITH ASPARAGUS I

1½ lbs. lean lamb　　　　　　2 cups fresh asparagus
1 small onion　　　　　　　　½ clove garlic
1 cup beef stock　　　　　　　1 teaspoon salt and dash pepper
4 tablespoons oil
SAUCE:
1 tablespoon cornflour　　　　1 tablespoon soy sauce

Cut the asparagus into sections about an inch long and discard the tough ends. Cut the lamb into thin small slices.

Heat a frying pan and put in the oil. When hot add the crushed garlic and the sliced onion. Fry until the onion starts to brown. Add the salt and pepper and then the lamb and fry briskly for 5 minutes. Then add the asparagus, cover, and reduce the flame. Cook for 5 minutes more then add the beef stock and continue cooking for 2 minutes. Mix the cornflour and soy sauce with a little water and add to the pan. Continue cooking until the sauce thickens and serve immediately.

LAMB WITH ASPARAGUS II

1 lb. lean lamb　　　　　　　asparagus
3 small tomatoes　　　　　　　½ cup beef stock
1 onion　　　　　　　　　　　4 tablespoons oil
1 teaspoon salt　　　　　　　　1 clove garlic
SAUCE:
1 tablespoon cornflour　　　　4 tablespoons water
2 teaspoons soy sauce

Cut enough asparagus in one-inch sections to fill two cups, and boil for 5 minutes. Cut the lamb into slices about an eighth of

an inch thick. Heat a frying pan and add the oil and salt with
a dash of pepper. When the oil is hot add the lamb and the
crushed garlic and sauté for about 10 minutes by which time
the lamb should be tender. Add to the lamb the cooked
asparagus, the tomatoes cut into quarters and the beef stock.
Cook over a moderate flame for 2 minutes. Blend together the
cornflour, soy sauce and water and pour this over the lamb and
vegetables. Cook over moderate flame until the sauce thickens
and serve immediately.

STEWED LAMB

2 lbs. of leg of lamb
6 tablespoons soy sauce
1 teaspoon salt

3 spring onions
1 tablespoon chopped ginger

Cut the lamb into inch cubes and put into a heavy saucepan
and cover with water. Bring to the boil and then add the soy
sauce, onions (cut in inch lengths), the ginger and the salt.
Cover and simmer gently for about 2 hours, adding a little
chicken stock if too much water evaporates. Serve hot. As no
vegetables are included in this be sure to serve it with hot
boiled rice.

FRIED LAMB

1½ lbs. lean lamb
2 tablespoons soy sauce
1 teaspoon salt

2 spring onions
1 tablespoon sherry
2 tablespoons oil

Cut the lamb into thin small slices and mix thoroughly in the
soy sauce, sherry, salt and onions.

Heat a frying pan and add the oil. When the oil is very hot
put in the lamb slices and fry, stirring constantly, for 3
minutes. Serve immediately.

LAMB WITH STRING BEANS

1 *lb. lean lamb*   1 *cup chicken stock*
1 *lb. string beans*   2 *tablespoons oil*
1 *teaspoon salt*
SAUCE:
2 *tablespoons cornflour*   4 *tablespoons water*
2 *teaspoons soy sauce*

Slice the beans and cook in boiling water for 5 minutes or until almost tender. Cut the lamb into thin slices. Heat a heavy frying pan and add 2 tablespoons of oil, 1 teaspoon of salt and a dash of pepper. Add the lamb slices and cook over a moderate flame until the meat is browned, stirring constantly. Then add the chicken stock and cook gently for 10 minutes, under a cover. Add the beans and the cornflour, soy sauce and water previously blended together. Cook for 5 minutes more, still stirring frequently and serve when the sauce has thickened.

LAMB WITH BROCCOLI

Proceed as in the previous recipe, substituting broccoli for string beans.

JELLIED LAMB

1½ lbs. shoulder of lamb   2 spring onions
1 clove garlic   3 tablespoons sherry
5 tablespoons soy sauce   2 teaspoons brown sugar
gelatine

With a cleaver cut the lamb into pieces about three inches by
two and drop them into boiling water. Cook for about 4
minutes. Pour off the water and add to the pot the onions
(chopped in sections), the garic (bruised), sugar, sherry and
soy sauce. Return enough of the water to the pot to barely
cover the ingredients. Simmer for at least 2 hours so that the
meat is thoroughly tender. Pour off the liquid, remove the
lamb and discard everything else Shared the meat from the
bones.

Soak a suitable quantity of gelatine (one tablespoon should
be enough) in half a cup of water for a few minutes and then
add ¾ of a cup of very hot water and stir until all the gelatine
is dissolved. Reheat the lamb stock, add the dissolved gelatine
and stir constantly until it boils. Add to it the shredded meat
and cook for 5 minutes, stirring frequently. Pour into a
shallow pan and chill until the whole thing is set and is a firm
jelly. To serve remove any fat and cut into slices about two
inches long by one and a quarter inch thick. If you have a
refrigerator this can be kept for several days. Slices of this
jellied lamb are sometimes served as cold hors d'oeuvre at the
beginning of a meal.

BARBECUED MUTTON

2 *lbs. lean mutton, preferably*   *bread rolls*
    from the saddle
SAUCE:
1 *tablespoon finely chopped*   1 *tablespoon sesame oil*
    ginger   1 *tablespoon sugar*
2 *cloves garlic, finely chopped*   ½ *cup vinegar*
4 *spring onions, finely chopped*   2 *tablespoons soy bean paste*
1 *teaspoon salt*   2 *tablespoons soy sauce*
½ *teaspoon white pepper*   2 *tablespoons finely chopped*
1 *red cayenne pepper finely*   *sweet pepper*
    chopped

This was generally known in Peking as Mongolian grilled mutton and was eaten out of doors during the winter round a big charcoal grill or barbecue. Over the glowing charcoal was a concave arrangement of thin iron strips, rather like a wire mesh.

Slice the mutton across the grain as thin as possible with a sharp knife, an eighth of an inch or even thinner. Arrange these slices on four plates and distribute round the grill. Mix all the sauce ingredients well together and divide it into four bowls, placing one beside each dish of mutton.

Take the bread rolls, about the size and shape of small hot cross buns, and cut them sideways half-way through. With the fingers or a fork scoop out the soft bread interior leaving a hollow crusty shell.

With chopsticks take several slices of mutton and soak them for a minute or two in the bowl of sauce. Then lay them on top of the grill. When they are cooked and sizzling hot stuff them into the hollow roll and eat.

If you wish, dip the cooked mutton in the sauce once more on its journey from grill to roll.

¶ LIVER

The most popular liver in China is the duck liver, which comes from the duck specially fattened for the Peking Duck dish (page 53), superior to chicken livers but not so rich as goose liver. Goose liver would be a good substitute when obtainable but chicken and calf liver will do very well.

DUCK LIVER ROLL

4 duck livers sliced finely
½ cup sliced water chestnuts
1 small onion sliced
4 tablespoons peanut oil
1 tablespoon sherry
1 tablespoon cornflour
3 tablespoons water

½ cup bamboo shoot, sliced
¼ cup sliced mushrooms
2 cups flour
3 tablespoons soy sauce
½ cup sugar
2 cups oil
salt to taste

Heat a frying pan and put in 4 tablespoons of oil. Scald the liver slices and sauté them. Add onion, salt, soy sauce, sherry, and sugar and sauté for a few seconds. Then add the mushrooms, bamboo shoot and water chestnuts and fry for 1 minute. Add 1 tablespoon of water just before removing from the fire. Mix the cornflour with a little water and stir into the mixture.

Make a dough from the flour with a little water, and roll out very thin indeed. Cut it into four rectangles. Put a generous amount of the cooked mixture on each rectangle and roll up and seal.

Heat a frying pan, add oil generously and fry the rolls until they are light brown. Place them on a dish and cut into pieces about two inches long. Serve piping hot.

FRIED LIVERS

4 *duck or* 8 *chicken livers*
  soaked in mixture of 2 *table-*
  spoons soy sauce and 1 *table-*
  spoon sherry
2 *cups oil*

½ *cup flour*
⅓ *cup water*
saltspoon of baking powder

Mix the flour, water and baking powder and then mix the livers in the flour mixture. Heat a frying pan and add the oil. When hot add the livers and fry for 2 minutes by which time they should be brown. Place on a plate and sprinkle with Chinese pepper (*Hua Chiao Mien-erh*) or ordinary pepper. Serve hot.

LIVER ON TOAST

4 *duck or* 8 *chicken livers finely*
  chopped
10 *water chestnuts, chopped*
½ *teaspoon salt*
20 *pieces bread* 2 *inches square*

1 *egg white*
1 *tablespoon soy sauce*
1 *teaspoon sherry*
2 *cups oil*

Mix together the chopped livers and water chestnuts and add to them the unbeaten egg white, then the soy sauce, the wine and salt. Pyramid the mixture on the squares of bread, decorate with chopped parsley and fry in deep fat until brown and crisp.

SHREDDED LIVER

1 *lb. calf's liver*
2 *tablespoons oil*

3 *tablespoons soy sauce*
salt to taste

Marinate the liver in soy sauce and oil for about an hour. Heat a frying pan and gently cook the liver in the marinating sauce and salt. When it is cooked through but not too well done remove the liver and grate it on a fairly fine grater. The result should be a light and fluffy mass. Place on a dish, sprinkle with Chinese pepper and serve.

SWEET AND SOUR CHICKEN LIVERS

½ lb. chicken livers	2 slices pineapple
2 green peppers	⅓ cup chicken stock
2 tablespoons oil	½ teaspoon salt and dash pepper
SAUCE:	
2 tablespoons cornflour	¼ cup sugar or honey
1 tablespoon soy sauce	½ cup chicken stock
¼ cup vinegar	

Into a hot frying pan put the oil, salt and pepper and when the oil is hot add the chicken livers, each cut into two or three pieces. Cook over a moderate flame, stirring constantly, until the livers are browned. Remove, and drain.

To what oil remains in the pan add ⅓ cup of chicken stock and then add the peppers, cut into pieces about an inch square, and the pineapple slices, each cut into six pieces. Cover the pan and cook over a moderate flame for 6 minutes. Uncover and add the chicken livers and the sauce ingredients, well blended. Cook slowly until the sauce thickens and clarifies. Serve immediately.

CALF LIVER AND CUCUMBER I

1 *lb. calf liver*
2 *teaspoons cornflour*
1 *teaspoon salt*
dash pepper
4 *tablespoons oil*

4 *small cucumbers*
1 *tablespoon chopped spring*
  onions
2 *tablespoons oil*
1 *teaspoon salt*
½ *cup chicken stock*

Slice liver about quarter of an inch thick and put into a bowl in which the cornflour, 1 teaspoon of salt, dash pepper and 4 tablespoons of oil have been mixed.

In a hot frying pan put 2 tablespoons of oil, 1 teaspoon salt and pepper. Add the liver and cook until brown over moderate heat. Stir frequently so the liver doesn't stick.

Cut the cucumbers lengthwise into four parts, remove the seeds and then slice diagonally in fairly thick slices and add them to the liver with the chicken stock. Cover the pan and cook until cucumbers are tender, about 4 minutes. When done sprinkle over the dish the chopped onions and serve hot, with boiled rice.

CALF LIVER AND CUCUMBER II

1 *lb. calf's liver*　　　　4 *small cucumbers*
1 *spring onion*　　　　　½ *cup chicken stock*
2 *teaspoons cornflour*　　1 *teaspoon salt*
dash of pepper　　　　　6 *tablespoons oil*

Wash the liver, remove any skin and then cut into slices about a third of an inch thick. Mix together 2 teaspoons cornflour, ½ teaspoon salt and a little pepper. Add 4 tablespoons of oil and when well blended pour this over the sliced liver, turning it so that it gets well covered. Leave for 2 or 3 minutes.

Heat a frying pan and add the rest of the oil, ½ teaspoon salt and a little pepper. When the oil is hot fry the liver slices until they are well browned.

Quarter the cucumbers lengthwise, remove all seeds and then slice diagonally, about a quarter of an inch thick. Add the cucumber to the pan together with the chicken stock and cook over a moderate flame for 4 minutes. Slice the onion thinly and add to the pan and continue cooking for 1 minute, stirring again. Return the liver to the pan for 10 seconds and serve immediately.

FISH

SWEET AND SOUR FISH

1 *fish about 2 lb.*	1 *white turnip*
1 *carrot*	1 *small onion*
3 *tablespoons oil*	
CORNFLOUR PASTE:	
3 *tablespoons cornflour*	2 *tablespoons water*
SWEET AND SOUR SAUCE:	
2 *tablespoons oil*	1 *cup vinegar*
½ *cup sugar or honey*	1 *tablespoon cornflour*
4 *tablespoons soy sauce*	

The fish can be either from fresh or salt water but not a flat
fish. Leave on head and tail but clean the inside thoroughly.
With a sharp knife make diagonal slashes on both sides from
head to tail and about an inch apart. Smear the fish well on
both sides with the cornflour paste. Heat a frying pan and put
in the oil. When it is very hot hold the fish over the pan by
the head and baste it with the hot oil until the exposed flesh in
the slashes is brown. Then drop the fish into the pan and fry
until it is crisp on the outside. Remove fish and drain.

Heat the pan again and put in 2 tablespoons of oil. Slice
the onion, dice the carrot and turnip and fry them for 1 minute.
Mix the sweet-sour ingredients and pour over the vegetables
and boil for 1 minute. Place the fish on a warm serving dish
and pour contents of pan over it. Serve immediately.

FRIED CARP WITH GINGER

1 3-*lb. carp*	5 *slices ginger*
2 *spring onions*	4 *tablespoons soy sauce*
3 *tablespoons sherry*	½ *teaspoon sugar*
1 *teaspoon salt*	2 *tablespoons flour*
1 *cup oil*	

Clean the fish but leave head and tail on. Slash the sides of the
fish and then rub the fish on both sides with dry flour. Heat a
frying pan and put in the oil, which should be not less than an
inch deep. When the oil is hot fry the fish in it, 1 minute to
each side. Then lower the flame and cook for 5 minutes more,
turning the fish half-way through the period. Pour off the oil
and add to the fish the soy sauce, sherry, sugar, salt, ginger
slices, chopped onion and about a cup of water. Cover and
cook over brisk heat for about 10 minutes. Serve hot.

FRIED PERCH, MULLET OR BASS

1 *fish about 2 lb.*	1 *spring onion*
4 *tablespoons soy sauce*	4 *tablespoons oil*
1 *teaspoon sugar*	1 *teaspoon salt*
3 *slices fresh ginger*	

Clean the fish, leaving on head and tail, and smear it both sides
with some of the soy sauce. Heat a frying pan and add the oil
and when hot fry the fish about a minute on each side, taking
care it doesn't stick to the bottom. Then add the onion
(chopped), ginger, soy sauce, salt, sugar and about ¾ cup of
water. Cover and cook gently for 10 minutes.

STEAMED FISH WITH EGGS

1½ *lbs. of fillet sole or*
flounder
1 *spring onion*
1 *tablespoon oil*
1 *tablespoon soy sauce*

4 *eggs*
1 *cup chicken stock*
1 *small green pepper*
1 *tablespoon cornflour*
1 *teaspoon salt*

Slice the fillets across, about ¾-inch wide, and place in a dish or shallow casserole. Blend thoroughly and sprinkle over the fish the oil, cornflour and soy sauce. Chop the onion finely and add it to the fish. Chop the pepper finely and add 1 tablespoon of it to the fish. Beat the eggs and add to them the chicken stock and the salt and then pour over the fish. Place the dish over boiling water, cover it tightly and steam over a fairly low flame for at least an hour. Serve immediately.

FILLETED FISH WITH SWEET-SOUR SAUCE

3 *lbs. fish*
3 *tablespoons cornflour*
breadcrumbs
SAUCE:
2 *tablespoons oil*
¼ *cup chicken stock*
2 *tablespoons brown sugar*

2 *egg yolks*
1 *tablespoon sherry*
saltspoon salt

1 *tablespoon chopped ginger*
1 *tablespoon cornflour*

Get quite thick fillets of fish, which can be haddock, rock cod or flounder. On one side of each fillet cut deep gashes with a sharp knife in a criss-cross pattern. Mix the egg yolks with the sherry, salt and 3 tablespoons of cornflour. Roll the fillets in this mixture until they are well coated and then roll in fine breadcrumbs.

Heat a deep frying pan, half fill it with oil and heat until it is very hot, about 375 degrees. Fry the fish for 10 minutes by which time it should be a golden brown. Put aside and keep warm.

Put the sweet-sour sauce ingredients into a saucepan, first mixing the cornflour with a little water, and stir over a moderate flame until it is smooth and slightly thickened. Pour it over the fish and serve immediately.

HADDOCK SAUTÉ

1 lb. fresh haddock filleted
2 slices ginger
2 spring onions
1 tablespoon vinegar
½ cup oil
1 tablespoon cornflour

6 medium mushrooms
1 clove garlic
1 bamboo shoot
¼ cup sherry
salt to taste

Peel the mushrooms, discarding the stalks, and then cut them in quarters. Cut the fish into pieces about an inch and a half square and dust them with cornflour. Heat a frying pan and add the oil. When it is hot fry the ginger and garlic in it for 1 minute, then add the haddock and sauté for about 2 minutes. Place the fish on one side and keep warm.

Add to the pan the chopped onions, half a cup of sliced bamboo shoot, the mushrooms, vinegar, sherry and salt. Cook these for 2 minutes over a moderate flame, stirring constantly. Then add half a teaspoon of cornflour mixed in a little water. Return the haddock to the pan and cook all ingredients together for another 2 minutes. Serve immediately.

There are variations to this dish. Other fish can be used (sole is very good indeed) and in place of sherry the cook can use any sweet wine, such as madeira and sweet sauternes. Sauternes and sole make a very good combination.

STEAMED FLOUNDER

1½ lbs. fillet of flounder
1 cup chicken stock
½ green pepper
1 tablespoon cornflour
1 teaspoon salt

4 eggs
1 spring onion
1 tablespoon oil
1 teaspoon soy sauce
dash pepper

Cut the flounder across the grain in half-inch slices and place these in a baking dish. Blend together the oil, cornflour, and soy sauce, and sprinkle it over the fish. Chop the onion finely and chop finely enough green pepper to make a heaping tablespoon and sprinkle these over the fish.

Beat the eggs and then stir in the stock, with the salt and a dash of pepper. When thoroughly mixed pour over the fish. Cover tightly. Half fill a roasting pan with water and put the dish containing the fish in it on a rack and cook in the oven for about an hour. The dish can also be placed over a saucepan of boiling water and steamed on top of the stove for 1 hour.

FRIED FISH WITH LILY BUDS

1 lb. fish fillets
1 tablespoon cornflour
12 day lily buds
salt to taste

1 spring onion, chopped
1 tablespoon water
½ cup oil

Almost any fish can be used for this dish but flounder, fresh haddock and sole are very good. Cut the fish across the grain into half an inch pieces. Mix the cornflour and water together and pour over the fish. Stir so that all gets smeared. Heat a frying pan and add the oil and when hot fry the chopped onion and the salt for a few seconds. Add the fish and sauté for 3 minutes, stirring constantly. Wash the lily buds, which should not be bigger than two inches long, and add to the pan.

Continue frying and turning for 3 minutes more and serve immediately.

If sauce is desired with this dish, remove the contents of the pan when cooked to a warm serving dish. To the pan add 2 tablespoons of soy sauce, 2 teaspoons of cornflour, ½ teaspoon of salt, 3 tablespoons of chicken stock and 1 tablespoon of sherry. Cook until it thickens, stirring constantly, and pour over the fish and serve.

Second method: Do not cut the fish but smear both sides of each fillet with cornflour and water mixture. Heat the pan, add the oil and when hot fry the chopped onion for 30 seconds. Then add the salt and the fish and fry to a golden brown on both sides. When the fish is turned to brown the other side add the lily buds. When done remove, drain and serve. If sauce is needed proceed as directed above.

STEAMED FISH WITH SOYA BEANS

1½ *lbs. fish*	1 *onion, sliced*
1 *teaspoon chopped ginger*	2 *tablespoons black salted soya*
¼ *clove garlic*	*beans*
	1 *tablespoon oil*

SAUCE:

2 *tablespoons soy sauce*	½ *teaspoon salt*
2 *tablespoons sherry*	1 *teaspoon sugar*

Use one fish. Clean it well and cover it well with the sauce mixture and place in a dish. Sprinkle over it the soya beans, the chopped ginger, the pounded garlic and the oil. Cover it tightly and steam over boiling water for 20 to 30 minutes, depending on the size of the fish.

FRIED CARP

1 *carp about 3 lbs.*	2 *spring onions*
fresh ginger	6 *tablespoons soy sauce*
2 *tablespoons sherry*	1 *teaspoon sugar*
1 *teaspoon salt*	1 *cup water*
flour	1 *cup oil*

Clean the fish but leave head and tail on. Slash the fish in a criss-cross fashion on both sides. Dust it well with flour. Heat a frying pan and add the oil and when it is quite hot put the fish in and fry each side for 2 minutes. Reduce the heat and continue frying for 5 minutes, turning the fish half way through this period. Drain off the oil and return one tablespoon to the pan. Add the soy sauce, sherry, salt and four or five thin slices of ginger root. Finally add the onions, cut into inch pieces, and then the sugar. Cover the pan and cook over a fairly brisk flame for 8 or 10 minutes. Serve hot immediately, pouring the liquid contents of the pan over the fish.

Various fish can be cooked by this method. Carp is preferred by Chinese above all other fish but mullet, perch, haddock and codling—indeed almost any fish—can be cooked in this way.

STEAMED FISH

1 *2-lb. fish*	*small piece fresh ginger*
1 *small onion*	1 *mushroom*
SAUCE:	
1 *tablespoon sherry*	1 *teaspoon cornflour*
1 *teaspoon sugar*	½ *teaspoon salt*
3 *tablespoons soy sauce*	

Clean the fish and smear it inside and out with the sauce mixture. Place it on a dish and garnish it with slices of mushroom, ginger and onion. Place the dish on a rack in a pan of hot water and cook gently until done. Alternatively put the fish in the perforated top of a double boiler or above the water in an asparagus cooker.

PINEAPPLE SOLE

1½ lbs. sole, filleted	2 eggs
small tin pineapple	2 tablespoons soy sauce
1 tablespoon sherry	2 spring onions
½ teaspoon salt	½ teaspoon sugar
2 teaspoons cornflour	3 tablespoons oil

Cut each fillet of fish across the grain into pieces an inch wide. Chop the onions finely and mix with the soy sauce, sherry and salt. Into this mixture put the pieces of fish and soak them for a few minutes.

Heat a heavy frying pan and add the oil. In the meantime mix the cornflour with the beaten eggs. Dip the fish pieces in the egg mixture and fry them for 3 or 4 minutes, turning occasionally so that each side is cooked.

Remove the fish and keep on a warm dish. Then add the sugar and two or three tablespoons of water to the egg and cornflour mixture in which the fish was dipped. Cut the pineapple slices into four pieces and dip them in the egg mixture. Then put egg mixture and pineapple into the frying pan, reduce the heat and cook until the sauce thickens and clears. Pour all over the fish and serve immediately.

FRIED SOLE WITH EGG

1½ lbs. filleted sole	3 eggs
1 spring onion	2 slices fresh ginger
2 tablespoons cornflour	1 tablespoon sherry
1 teaspoon salt	4 tablespoons oil

Cut each fillet into quarters. Lightly beat the eggs and add ½ teaspoon of salt and the cornflour. When this is smooth, dip the fish pieces in it so that they are well covered. Heat a frying pan and add the oil. When it is hot fry the fish for 4 minutes, turning once in the process.

To what is left of the egg mixture add the sherry, the rest of the salt, the onion (chopped), the ginger (chopped), and about 2 tablespoons of water. When well blended add to the fish in the pan and cook until the sauce thickens, about 2 minutes, turning the fish three or four times during the process. Serve immediately.

Fresh haddock can be substituted for sole if the latter is not available.

SMOKED FISH I

1½ lbs. filleted fish	2 spring onions
5 slices ginger	½ clove garlic
2 tablespoons soy sauce	1 tablespoon sherry
1 teaspoon sesame oil	1 teaspoon sugar
1 cup oil	salt to taste
SAUCE:	
2 teaspoons soy sauce	½ teaspoon salt
½ teaspoon sugar	⅓ cup chicken stock

Chop the onions finely and add to them the ginger, soy sauce, sesame oil, the garlic, sherry, sugar and salt. Cut the fish fillets in half across the grain and soak them in this mixture for not less than half an hour. Heat a frying pan and add the oil. When it is very hot fry the fish to a light golden brown.

Remove the fish. Pour off the oil except for about 3 tablespoons. Add the sauce mixture to the pan and then the fish. Continue cooking until the sauce has practically evaporated and serve the fish immediately. The fish should be a lovely dark brown as if it had been smoked.

SMOKED FISH II

1½ lbs. filleted fish	2 tablespoons soy sauce
1 spring onion	2 teaspoons sesame oil
1 tablespoon sherry	1 teaspoon chopped ginger
1 teaspoon sugar	salt and pepper to taste

Only attempt this if you don't mind the kitchen being enveloped in a cloud of smoke. The best fish to use is Mandarin fish, if available, but almost any filleted fish will do. Cut each fillet into pieces about four inches long and two or three inches wide. Mix all the other ingredients together and marinate the fish for about 15 minutes.

Place the fillets on a shallow pan (something like a biscuit sheet) and add a little of the sauce in which they were marinated. Put the pan on the top shelf of the oven and bake in a moderate heat for 15 minutes.

Have prepared a shallow baking tin half full of sawdust. Drop a small live coal into this and place on the bottom shelf of the oven. Continue baking the fish for 5 minutes more. The smoke will fill the oven and 'cure' the fish while cooking. Dispose of the smouldering sawdust quickly and serve the fish immediately.

SMOKED FISH III

1½ *lbs. filleted fish*   2 *teaspoons salt*
3 *tablespoons brown sugar*   4 *tablespoons oil*

Rub the salt into both sides of the fish and leave for an hour. Heat a frying pan and add the oil. When it is hot fry the fillets for 10 minutes, 5 on each side.

Place the fish on a rack in a shallow baking tin and put the brown sugar on the baking tin under the fish. Turn the oven heat to high and leave for 5 minutes. The smoke from the burning sugar will smoke the fish. Serve immediately.

ABALONE

Abalone is a shell fish in a deep shell, about six to eight inches long and four or five inches wide. The shell is beautifully iridescent. The fish is of a rubbery texture but delicious when properly cooked. Abalone steak is common in restaurants on the west coast of the United States, and China used to import most of its abalone from California.

In the Channel Islands there is a variety of abalone known as ormers; in Britain abalone are sometimes available in tins.

BRAISED ABALONE

1 16 oz. tin abalone
6 mushrooms
2 cups chicken stock
1 small onion
4 tablespoons soy sauce
1 tablespoon cornflour mixed
  with 2 tablespoons water

4 water chestnuts
1 bamboo shoot
½ cup water from abalone
½ teaspoon salt
1 teaspoon sherry
small piece ginger

Put the sliced mushrooms, ½ cup of sliced bamboo shoot, the chopped onion, sliced water chestnuts and two or three slices of ginger in the chicken stock and simmer down until about half the stock remains. Then add the water from the abalone tin. Add the salt, soy sauce ,sherry and sugar and bring to the boil.

Slice the abalone about an eighth of an inch thick and add to the stock and bring to the boil again. Then add the cornflour paste and cook for two minutes. Serve hot.

BOILED FRESH ABALONE

3 *abalones*
½ *lb. lean pork*
SAUCE:
2 *tablespoons soy sauce*
1 *teaspoon salt*

2 *cups chicken stock*

1 *teaspoon cornflour*

Cover the abalones with water and soak for at least 24 hours. Then wash them thoroughly and put in a saucepan with 4 cups of cold water. Bring to the boil and boil briskly for half an hour. Drain the abalones and return to the saucepan with 2 cups of water and the chicken stock and the pork and simmer gently until the abalones are tender. Remove the abalones and pork and save the stock. Slice the abalones, about a quarter of an inch thick, and arrange on a warm serving dish. Add the soy sauce, cornflour and salt to the stock, simmer for 5 seconds and pour over the sliced abalone and serve immediately.

CANTONESE LOBSTER

2 *small lobsters*
1 *cup chicken stock*
1 *stalk celery*
2 *tablespoons oil*
1 *egg*
2 *teaspoons soy sauce*

½ *lb. lean pork*
1 *carrot*
1 *spring onion*
1½ *teaspoons salt*
2 *tablespoons cornflour*

Cook two live lobsters in boiling water for 5 minutes. Remove and cut each big claw into two pieces and crack. Cut the body down the centre and with a cleaver cut each half into three pieces, leaving the shell attached.

Mince the pork coarsely and add to it 1 tablespoon diced carrot, another of diced celery and the chopped-up onion. Add half a teaspoon of salt and a dash of pepper. Place pork and vegetables in a pre-heated frying pan in which 2 table-spoons of oil and 1 teaspoon of salt have been made hot. Add the lobster and the chicken stock and cook briskly for half a minute. Cover the pan and reduce the flame to low and continue cooking gently for 10 minutes. Uncover and add the slightly beaten egg and cook over a high flame for a minute, stirring constantly. Blend together the cornflour, soy sauce and a quarter of a cup of water and add this to the pan. Continue cooking over a moderate flame until the sauce thickens. Place the pieces of lobster in a warm serving dish and then cover with the sauce and serve immediately.

'DRAGON SHRIMP'

2 *small lobsters*	2 *eggs*
2 *ozs. minced pork*	1 *spring onion*
2 *tablespoons sherry*	2 *tablespoons soy sauce*
2 *tablespoons cornflour*	1 *teaspoon salt*
3 *teaspoons chopped ginger*	3 *tablespoons oil*

In China lobsters are small and often called 'dragon shrimp'. Drop the lobsters into boiling water and cook for 5 minutes if they are very small (1 lb.) or a bit longer if they are bigger.

Remove and, when cool, split the body in two and then each half into three pieces (with shell on). Split the big claws into two or three pieces each. Discard the rest.

Chop the onion finely and mix with ginger, sherry, soy sauce, salt, pork, the eggs lightly beaten and the cornflour mixed with a little water.

Heat a heavy frying pan and add the oil. When it is hot put the pieces of lobster in and then pour the sauce mixture over the top. Cook over a moderate flame for 6 minutes and serve immediately.

LOBSTER WITH VEGETABLES

½ *lb. lobster meat*   1 *lb. green peas*
1 *cup diced carrots*   ½ *cup diced green pepper*
½ *cup diced celery*   ½ *clove garlic*
2 *tablespoons chopped onion*   1 *cup chicken stock*
3 *tablespoons oil*   ½ *teaspoon salt*
                                     ½ *teaspoon sugar*

SAUCE:
2 *tablespoons cornflour*   ¼ *cup water*
2 *teaspoons soy sauce*

Shell the peas and boil with the carrots for 5 minutes. Drain
and put aside. Heat a frying pan, add the oil and when hot
add the salt, a dash of pepper, the garlic, green pepper and
celery and fry for 5 seconds. Add the stock and the sugar and
then the lobster meat cut into half-inch sections. Cook over a
moderate flame for 5 minutes, stirring constantly. Add the
cooked peas and carrots and fry for 5 seconds.

Blend the sauce ingredients and add to the pan and, stirring
constantly, cook until the sauce thickens and the whole dish is
hot. Serve immediately.

FRIED OYSTERS

24 *oysters*   6 *slices bacon*
1 *egg*   6 *tablespoons oil*
⅔ *cup chopped onion*
SAUCE:
1 *tablespoon cornflour*   ½ *cup beef stock*
1 *teaspoon soy sauce*

Remove oysters from the shell. Cut the bacon in pieces two
inches long and lay an oyster on each piece of bacon. Beat the
egg with 1 tablespoon of water and dip each oyster in it. Heat

a frying pan, add the oil and when hot put the oysters carefully in and brown both sides. Remove and place them on a warm serving dish. Leave 2 tablespoons of oil in the pan and fry the onion golden brown then add the sauce mixture and cook until it thickens. Then pour over the oysters and serve them immediately.

FRIED SCALLOPS I

1 *lb. scallops*
1 *cup chicken stock*
4 *tablespoons oil*
SAUCE:
2 *teaspoons cornflour*
2 *teaspoons soy sauce*

1 *lb. string beans*
2 *tomatoes*
1 *teaspoon salt*

¼ *cup water*

Slice the beans and boil them for 5 minutes. Drain and reserve. Heat a frying pan, add the oil and when hot add the salt and a dash of pepper. Dip the scallops in flour and add to the pan and cook until they are golden brown, stirring frequently. Add the stock to the pan and then the tomatoes, cut into eight pieces, and the cooked beans. Cook, still stirring, for 3 minutes.

Blend the sauce mixture, add to the pan and cook until the sauce thickens, stirring constantly. Serve immediately.

FRIED SCALLOPS II

1 *lb. scallops*	6 *ozs. mushrooms*
1 *spring onion*	3 *slices ginger*
2 *tablespoons soy sauce*	1 *teaspoon salt*
1 *teaspoon sugar*	3 *tablespoons oil*

Clean the scallops and if they are large cut in half across the grain. Quarter the mushrooms if they are small or cut into six wedges if they are large.

Heat a frying pan and add the oil. When hot put in the scallops and fry for 2 minutes, stirring constantly. Then add the mushrooms, the onion (chopped into inch pieces), the ginger, soy sauce, salt and sugar. Continue cooking over a moderate flame for 2 minutes. Serve hot immediately.

If the scallops are very large continue the first frying for a little while.

SCALLOPS WITH EGGS

¾ *lb. scallops*	2 *eggs*
4 *tablespoons oil*	1 *tablespoon sherry*
saltspoon each of sugar and salt	
and dash of pepper	

Wash the scallops, which should be small ones, and put in 4 tablespoons of oil heated in a frying pan. Sauté for 3 minutes, browning them slightly on both sides. Add to the pan the sherry, salt and pepper and continue cooking for 1 minute, stirring frequently. Separate yolks and whites of the eggs and beat together two yolks and one white. When this is smooth pour it over the scallops, turn up the flame and cook briskly for 2 minutes, stirring frequently. The cooked egg will cover each scallop. Serve hot.

The appearance of the dish is improved if a little shredded ham is sprinkled over the dish before it is taken to the table.

CRAB OMELETTE

1 *cup flaked crab meat*   ½ *cup shredded bamboo shoot*
½ *cup shredded celery*   ½ *cup shredded onion*
4 *eggs*   2 *tablespoons soy sauce*
1 *teaspoon salt*   1½ *tablespoons flour*
dash pepper   3 *tablespoons oil*

Heat a frying pan and add the oil. When hot fry the vegetables
for 1 minute and then remove to a bowl. Add to them the crab
meat, the lightly beaten eggs, soy sauce, salt, pepper and the
flour. Mix thoroughly.

Reheat the pan and add 1 tablespoon of oil. When hot drop
the omelette mixture in, a tablespoonful at a time, and fry
until light brown on both sides. Serve immediately.

FROGS' LEGS SAUTÉ

4 *mushrooms*
2 *spring onions*
1 *lb. small frogs' legs*
¼ *cup chicken stock*
½ *teaspoon sugar*
4 *tablespoons oil*
1 *tablespoon sherry*

1 *small green pepper*
6 *water chestnuts*
½ *clove garlic*
2 *or 3 slices fresh ginger*
1 *teaspoon cornflour*
salt to taste

Divide the frogs' legs and if they are large cut each leg in two. Heat the oil in a frying pan and sauté the frogs' legs with garlic and ginger for 2 minutes. Then add the chopped onions and the sherry and cook for another 3 minutes. Remove the frogs' legs, garlic and ginger, discarding the garlic and ginger and keeping the frogs' legs warm. Slice the mushrooms and water chestnuts and cut the pepper into pieces an inch square. Add all three ingredients to the hot oil and cook for two minutes.

Remove the vegetables and put them with the frogs' legs. To the oil in the pan add the chicken stock, the sugar and the cornflour, mixed with a little water. Cook this sauce over a moderate flame until it is smooth and slightly thickened. Add to it frogs' legs and vegetables and cook briskly for 2 minutes, stirring frequently. Serve immediately.

SHRIMPS

Shrimps vary enormously in various parts of the world. In China they are very large indeed, much bigger than English prawns. I have often seen them, still with head and tail, at least eight inches long. In the shrimp recipes the quantities, where numbers are given, have been altered from the original recipes and they refer to shrimps about the size of an English prawn. Where possible quantities are given in weight.

BUTTERFLY SHRIMPS

1 lb. shrimps or prawns
oil for deep frying
1 teaspoon salt
MARINATING SAUCE:
2 tablespoons sherry
½ teaspoon salt
2 tablespoons soy sauce

1 egg
4 tablespoons flour

1 chopped spring onion
1 teaspoon chopped ginger

The shrimps are shelled but their tails left on. Then split them down the middle almost to the tail. Marinate them for 5 minutes in the sauce, turning occasionally. Use a deep-frying saucepan with a wire basket as for French fried potatoes. Heat the oil to about 375 degrees. Lightly beat the egg and mix it smoothly with the flour. Remove the shrimps from the marinating sauce, roll them once in the egg and flour mixture and drop into the smoking oil in the wire basket. Fry for 3 minutes or as much as five according to the size of the shrimps. They are done when they are golden brown. Serve immediately. If the prawns or shrimps are bought ready cooked they will need to be fried for only a minute.

PHOENIX-TAIL SHRIMPS

1 *lb. shrimps*	2 *spring onions*
1 *slice ginger*	1 *clove garlic*
2 *tablespoons dry sherry*	2 *tablespoons chopped sweet*
4 *tablespoons oil*	*pickles*
SAUCE:	
3 *tablespoons soy sauce*	½ *teaspoon sugar*
2 *teaspoons cornflour*	

Shell the shrimps but leave the tails on. These turn red in cooking, hence the name of the dish. Wash them thoroughly and dry. Heat a frying pan and add the oil. When it is smoking hot add the onions cut in inch lengths, the ginger finely chopped and the garlic pounded to a pulp. Stir these in and then add the shrimp. Cook them for 2 minutes if they are small, or 3 if they are large. Stir them constantly. Then add the sherry and the pickle and continue cooking over a high flame for 1 minute. Remove the shrimps and put in a warm place.

Now add to the oil in the pan the soy sauce and sugar and the cornflour mixed with a little cold water. Cook the sauce over a moderate flame until it is smooth and thickened. Return the shrimps to the pan and cook for 30 seconds to heat them through again. Serve immediately.

Another version of this omits pickles, onions and ginger but includes a mixture of one egg, 4 tablespoons of flour and 4 tablespoons of water to make a batter in which the shrimps are dipped before being fried.

SHRIMPS WITH BACON

20 *large shrimps*   5 *slices bacon*
1 *egg*   1 *large onion, sliced*
1 *tablespoon water*   6 *tablespoons oil*
SAUCE:
1 *tablespoon cornflour*   ¾ *cup beef or chicken stock*
1 *teaspoon soy sauce*

Shell and clean the shrimps and cut the bacon into pieces an inch and a half long. Beat together the egg and 1 tablespoon water. Wrap a piece of bacon round each shrimp and dip in the egg mixture. Heat a frying pan and add the oil and when hot add the shrimps and cook over a moderate flame until brown on both sides. Remove the shrimps, drain and keep warm.

Leave 2 tablespoons of oil in the pan and add the onion and fry until golden brown. Blend the sauce mixture and add to the onions, cooking until it thickens, stirring constantly. Pour onions and sauce over the shrimps and serve immediately.

F

SHRIMPS WITH STRING BEANS

1 *lb. shrimps*
1 *cup chicken stock*
½ *teaspoon salt*
SAUCE:
2 *tablespoons cornflour*
2 *teaspoons soy sauce*

1 *lb. string beans*
4 *tablespoons oil*
dash of pepper

¼ *cup water*

Slice the beans and boil in salted water until almost tender. Do not overcook. Drain them. Shell the shrimps and cut into inch lengths. Heat a frying pan, add the oil, salt and pepper and when hot add the shrimps and cook over moderate flame until lightly brown. Then add the stock, cover the pan and simmer for 5 minutes. Open, add the beans and the blended sauce mixture. Cook, stirring constantly, until the sauce thickens and the beans are heated through. Serve immediately.

SHRIMPS WITH CUCUMBER

½ *lb. large shrimps*
2 *tablespoons oil*
1 *teaspoon sugar*
SAUCE:
1 *tablespoon cornflour*
½ *teaspoon salt*

2 *cucumbers*
2 *tablespoons soy sauce*
1 *teaspoon cornflour*

1 *tablespoon sherry*

Cut the cucumbers (with skin on) into quarters lengthwise and then each quarter into 1½ inch lengths. Shell the shrimps and soak them in the sauce mixture. Heat a frying pan and add the oil. When hot fry the shrimps for 5 seconds. Remove and drain.

Leave 1 tablespoon of oil in the pan, add the cucumbers and fry for 3 or 4 seconds then add the soy sauce, sugar and the cornflour mixed with a little water. Continue cooking for 1 minute then add the shrimps and cook for 30 seconds. Serve immediately.

SHRIMPS WITH VEGETABLES

1 *lb. shrimps*   ½ *cup bean sprouts*
5 *mushrooms*   2 *stalks celery*
10 *water chestnuts*   2 *medium onions*
1 *tablespoon cornflour*   3 *tablespoons oil*
SAUCE:
2 *tablespoons soy sauce*   1 *tablespoon sherry*
1 *tablespoon finely chopped*   ¼ *teaspoon salt*
   ginger

Shell the shrimps and soak them in the sauce mixture for a few
minutes. Heat a frying pan, add the oil and when hot fry
vegetables for 1 minute. The mushrooms should be sliced, the
water chestnuts quartered and the celery cut into inch lengths.
Then add the marinated shrimps and cook for 10 seconds. Mix
the cornflour with ⅓ cup of water, add to the pan and simmer
until the sauce thickens. Serve immediately.

FRIED SHRIMPS WITH WATER CHESTNUT

1½ *lbs. shrimps*
1 *clove garlic*
2 *spring onions*
½ *teaspoon salt*
SAUCE:
¾ *cup chicken stock*
½ *teaspoon sugar*
1 *teaspoon sherry*

2 *egg whites*
1 *cup water chestnuts*
1 *tablespoon sherry*
½ *cup oil*

¼ *teaspoon salt*
2 *teaspoons cornflour*

Shell and wash the shrimps and dry them in a cloth. Leave whole if they are small and cut in half if they are large. When dry roll them in the slightly beaten egg whites.

Heat a heavy frying pan, add half the oil and when it is hot fry the chopped garlic until it browns. Then add the onions, chopped into half-inch lengths, and then the shrimps. Keep the flame high and fry the shrimps, constantly turning, for 2 minutes. During this process add the sherry and the salt. Remove the shrimps when they are pink.

Add a little more oil if necessary and then fry the water chestnuts, cut into quarters, for about 2 minutes, stirring constantly. Finally add the sauce ingredients, blended together, and turn down the flame. Simmer, while stirring, until the sauce thickens. When it does, return the shrimps to the pan and keep simmering for 30 seconds. Serve immediately.

SHRIMP OMELETTE

1 lb. shrimps
3 eggs
2 tablespoons sherry
1 tablespoon soy sauce
1 teaspoon salt

4 ozs. minced pork
1 teaspoon chopped ginger
1 tablespoon cornflour
1 spring onion
4 tablespoons oil

Shell and wash the shrimps and dry them. If they are large cut them in half. Mix together the cornflour, sherry, soy sauce, chopped onion, ginger and salt. Add 1 tablespoon water and when smooth put the shrimps in and then the minced pork.

Heat a frying pan, add the oil and when it is hot fry the shrimps and pork for 4 minutes. Remove and add shrimps and pork to the lightly beaten eggs. Return all to the pan and cook for about 3 minutes. Serve immediately.

SHRIMP AND PORK BALLS

1 lb. fresh shrimps
1 tablespoon sherry
2 tablespoons soy sauce
1 teaspoon sugar
4 tablespoons oil

6 ozs. pork
1½ tablespoons cornflour
1 teaspoon salt
2 tablespoons water

Shell and clean the shrimps and put them through the mincer with the pork (which should be one third fat). Stir into the shrimp and pork mixture all the other ingredients (except the oil) after mixing the cornflour with the water. Stir until everything is thoroughly mixed and then form into balls about the size of a walnut. Flatten these until they are half an inch thick.

Heat a frying pan and add the oil. When it is quite hot put in the shrimp and pork balls, turn down the flame and cook gently for not less than six minutes, turning them several times in the process. Test one to make sure the interior is properly cooked. Serve hot immediately.

SHRIMP CROÛTONS

1 *lb. shrimps*
3 *slices white bread*
2 *egg whites*
3 *tablespoons soy sauce*
½ *teaspoon salt*

12 *water chestnuts*
1 *cup oil*
1 *tablespoon cornflour*
2 *tablespoons sherry*

Shell and clean the shrimps and smear with mixture of corn-flour, egg whites and 1 tablespoon of water. Heat a frying pan, add the oil and when it is hot fry the shrimps for 1 minute. Remove the shrimps and drain. Heat the pan again and return the drained oil and in this when very hot fry the bread, which should be cut into pieces two inches square. When brown place the bread on a warm serving dish. Reheat the pan and add 2 tablespoons of oil. Sauté the sliced water chestnuts for a minute and then add to them the shrimps. Continue cooking for 30 seconds and then add the soy sauce, sugar, salt and sherry. Then add 3 tablespoons of water, cook for a few seconds and pour over the bread croûtons and serve immediately.

FRIED SHRIMPS I

1 *lb. fresh shrimps*
fresh ginger
2 *tablespoons sherry*
1 *teaspoon salt*

1 *spring onion*
1 *tablespoon cornflour*
3 *tablespoons oil*

Shell and clean the shrimps and soak them for a minute in a mixture of the cornflour, salt, sherry, the onion (chopped finely) and a small nugget of ginger chopped finely.

Heat a frying pan, add the oil and make it very hot. Sauté the shrimps for 3 minutes over a hot flame or up to 5 minutes if they are very large. Serve hot.

If you wish, sliced bamboo shoots or water chestnuts can be added to this dish.

FRIED SHRIMPS II

1 *lb. fresh shrimps*   1 *egg*
2 *tablespoons flour*   ½ *teaspoon salt*
1 *large onion*   1 *cup oil*
SAUCE:
1 *tablespoon cornflour*   1 *tablespoon sherry*
1 *teaspoon soy sauce*   ½ *cup stock, chicken or beef*

Shell and clean the shrimps. Mix together the egg, flour and
salt to make a batter and pour this over the shrimps. Toss them
until they are well covered.

Heat a heavy frying pan and add the oil. When it is very hot
spear two or three shrimps on the prongs of a fork and drop
into the hot fat. Fry until they are golden brown. Don't put
the shrimps in all together as they will form a solid mass.

When all the shrimps are cooked pour off the oil and return
2 tablespoons to the pan. Chop the onion and fry to a golden
brown. Blend the sauce ingredients together and pour over the
onion and cook over a moderate flame until the sauce thickens.
Pour the sauce over the shrimps and serve immediately.

SHRIMPS WITH MUSHROOMS

1 *lb. shrimps*   1/2 *lb. mushrooms*
1/2 *cup chicken stock*   2 *tablespoons oil*
1 *teaspoon salt*   2 *tablespoons cornflour*
2 *teaspoons soy sauce*

Shell the shrimps and cut into two or three pieces, depending on size. Put them in a frying pan in which the oil and salt have been heated and cook for 4 minutes or until they are pink. Add the mushrooms, sliced, and the chicken stock. Cover the pan and cook over a low flame for 5 minutes.

Make a sauce of the cornflour, soy sauce and about 1/4 cup of water. Pour this over the shrimps and mushrooms and cook for 3 or 4 minutes until the sauce thickens. Stir throughout the cooking process. Serve hot.

SHRIMPS WITH LETTUCE

1 *lb. shrimps*   1 *cos lettuce*
1/2 *cup chicken stock*   3 *tablespoons oil*
1/2 *teaspoon salt*   1 *tablespoon cornflour*
2 *teaspoons soy sauce*

Shell the shrimps, clean and cut into inch sections. Heat a sauté pan, add the oil and salt and sauté the shrimps until they are all pink. Remove the outside leaves of the lettuce and slice across into half-inch sections. Add the lettuce and the stock to the shrimps and cook over a low flame for 3 minutes. Blend the cornflour, soy sauce and a little water and pour into the pan. Continue cooking for about 3 minutes or until the sauce thickens. Serve hot immediately.

PRAWNS WITH ASPARAGUS

8 *prawns*   12 *stalks asparagus*
small piece ginger root   2 *tablespoons soy sauce*
1 *teaspoon sugar*   1 *teaspoon sherry*
2 *tablespoons oil*   *salt to taste*

Shell the prawns and cut into half-inch lengths. Clean the
asparagus and cut diagonally into one-inch lengths and boil for
3 minutes. Strain and retain the water.

Heat a frying pan and add the oil. When hot sauté the prawns
until they turn pink. Then add the asparagus to the pan and the
sugar, sherry, soy sauce, salt, 2 tablespoons of the asparagus
water and a small piece of ginger chopped finely. Continue
cooking for half a minute and serve.

BRAISED PRAWNS

12 *prawns*   1 *small onion*
small piece ginger   1 *bamboo shoot or half*
3 *tablespoons oil*   *small cucumber*
4 *teaspoons sherry*   1 *teaspoon sugar*
                                    4 *tablespoons soy sauce*

Remove heads of prawns but retain shell and cut each prawn
into three pieces. Slice the vegetables lengthwise. Heat a
frying pan and add the oil and sauté the prawns until they turn
pink. Then add the soy sauce, the sugar and the sherry. Fry
for 30 seconds and then add the ginger, chopped fine, and the
vegetables and continue cooking for 30 seconds more. Add
about a quarter of a cup of water, cook for another 2 minutes
and serve hot.

FRIED SHRIMP BALLS

1 *lb. shrimps*   10 *water chestnuts*
1 *tablespoon sherry*   1 *egg*
2 *tablespoons cornflour*   ½ *teaspoon salt*
2 *cups oil*

Shell the shrimps and chop them finely. Chop the water chestnuts finely and mix with the shrimps. Then add the cornflour,
sherry, beaten egg and salt. After mixing thoroughly mould the
mixture into small balls, about three-quarters of an inch in
diameter. Heat a frying pan, add the oil and when quite hot
drop the shrimp balls in and fry to a golden brown. Serve
immediately.

FRIED SHRIMP CROÛTONS

1 *lb. shrimps*   10 *water chestnuts*
1 *egg*   1 *tablespoon sherry*
2 *tablespoons cornflour*   ½ *teaspoon salt*
15 *squares white bread*   1 *cup oil*

Proceed exactly as in the previous recipe but instead of making
balls of the mixture pyramid it on the squares of bread, which
should not be bigger than an inch and a half square. Make the
oil very hot and drop in the croûtons a few at a time and fry
until they are a golden brown.

FRIED SQUID

3 *small dried squid*
3 *slices fresh ginger*
2 *tablespoons sherry*
3 *tablespoons oil*

2 *spring onions*
2 *tablespoons soy sauce*
1 *tablespoon cornflour*

Steep the squid in warm water until they swell back to normal size. Clean them well. Cut the squid into inch squares and the tentacles into pieces about an inch and a half long.

Heat a frying pan and add the oil. When hot put the pieces of squid in together with the onions, cut into inch lengths, and the ginger. Fry over a moderate flame for about 3 minutes. Add to the pan the soy sauce and the sherry and continue cooking for 2 minutes. Remove the squid to a warm serving dish. To the sauce in the pan add the cornflour mixed with a little water. Cook this over a low flame until it thickens and then pour over the squid and serve.

VEGETABLES

BAMBOO SHOOTS AND MUSHROOMS

3 *bamboo shoots*	10 *mushrooms*
1 *tablespoon sherry*	1 *teaspoon sugar*
5 *tablespoons soy sauce*	½ *cup oil*

If the bamboo shoots are fresh, remove outside leaves and boil for 10 minutes. If tinned, they will be ready for use. Slice the bamboo shoots lengthwise to the shape of French fried potatoes. Remove stalks of mushrooms and slice the caps. Fry the bamboo shoot slices in 6 tablespoons of oil for 2 minutes, then drain and put aside. Fry the sliced mushrooms in 2 tablespoons of oil for 2 minutes then add the sugar, soy sauce and sherry and 4 tablespoons of water. Then return bamboo shoots to the pan and simmer for 15 minutes. Serve hot.

The Chinese usually use dried mushrooms. In that event soak them in water half an hour before slicing.

BEAN SPROUTS AND PORK

4 *cups bean sprouts*	¼ *lb. lean pork*
4 *tablespoons oil*	½ *teaspoon salt*
SAUCE:	
2 *tablespoons soy sauce*	1 *teaspoon sugar*
1 *tablespoon sherry*	½ *teaspoon salt*
1 *teaspoon cornflour*	

Cut the pork into very thin slices and soak it well in the sauce. Heat a frying pan, add the oil and when hot sauté the bean sprouts for 2 minutes, stirring constantly. Remove them, reheat the pan, add 2 tablespoons of oil and sauté the pork for 2 minutes. Then add the bean sprouts and the salt, cook for 5 seconds, stirring, and serve immediately.

LEEKS AND BAMBOO SHOOTS

1 *bunch leeks*   2 *bamboo shoots*
¼ *lb. lean pork*   3 *tablespoons oil*
SAUCE:
1 *tablespoon soy sauce*   ½ *teaspoon salt*
1 *teaspoon cornflour*   1 *teaspoon sherry*

Cut the pork in thin slices and add to the sauce. Soak for 2 or 3 minutes. Heat a frying pan, add the oil and fry 1 cup of bamboo shoots sliced finely, with the leeks cut into one-inch lengths and the pork. Sauté the whole thing for 1 minute over a hot flame and serve.

ASPARAGUS

12 *stalks tinned asparagus*   ¼ *cup chicken stock*
¼ *cup water from asparagus*   1 *tablespoon sherry*
½ *teaspoon salt*   2 *tablespoons soy sauce*
2 *tablespoons oil*   1 *tablespoon cornflour*

Heat a frying pan, add the oil and the water from the asparagus, the sherry, salt, soy sauce and cornflour. Stir constantly for 15 seconds. Add the asparagus and cook for 5 seconds. Remove asparagus and serve immediately.

STUFFED EGGPLANT

1 *large eggplant*
10 *water chestnuts*
small piece ginger
2 *tablespoons soy sauce*
1 *teaspoon sugar*

½ *lb. lean pork*
1 *small onion, chopped finely*
1 *tablespoon sherry*
½ *teaspoon salt*

Put the pork through a mincer and add to it the water chestnuts chopped finely, also the chopped onion and about a teaspoon of chopped ginger. Mix thoroughly and add the soy sauce, sherry, salt and sugar. Wash and peel the eggplant and cut in half, stuffing each half with the mixture. Place these in a large bowl, cover and steam for at least half an hour.

BEAN SPROUTS AND DUCK

1 *lb. bean sprouts*
2 *tablespoons oil*
2 *tablespoons soy sauce*

½ *lb. duck meat*
1 *tablespoon sherry*
½ *teaspoon salt*

This is for using up left-over duck. Boil the bean sprouts for 2 minutes and meanwhile shred the left-over duck. Heat a frying pan and add the oil. When hot, sauté the parboiled sprouts for a minute and then add the sherry, soy sauce, salt and 2 tablespoons of water. Stir and add in the shredded duck and cook for 1 minute.

MUSHROOMS AND WATER CHESTNUTS

12 *water chestnuts*   18 *mushrooms*
2 *tablespoons oil*   1 *tablespoon sherry*
1 *teaspoon sugar*   3 *tablespoons soy sauce*
½ *teaspoon salt*

Slice the mushrooms, not too finely, and then slice the water chestnuts very thinly. Heat a frying pan, add the oil and when it is hot put in the mushrooms, soy sauce, sherry, salt and sugar. Cook for 2 or 3 seconds. Then add the water chestnuts and about 1 tablespoon of water. Lower the flame and simmer gently until the mushrooms are tender. Serve immediately.

The Chinese frequently use dried mushrooms for this dish, indeed they use dried mushrooms much oftener than fresh for all dishes calling for this vegetable. If dried mushrooms are used soak them long enough to restore them to their normal proportions.

STRING BEANS

1 *lb. fresh string beans*   3 *tablespoons oil*
1 *teaspoon salt*

Wash the beans, remove heads and tails and then cut into pieces two inches long. Put the oil in a frying pan and when it is moderately hot put in the beans and cook for 1 minute. Then add the salt and about half a cup of water. Cover and cook gently for 2 minutes. Remove cover and cook for 5 minutes more, still stirring constantly. Serve immediately.

SPINACH

1½ *lbs. spinach*   2 *tablespoons oil*
1 *teaspoon salt*

Wash the spinach and shake well to remove excess water.
Heat a frying pan, add the oil and when it is hot add the spinach
(uncut) and the salt. Cook for 3 minutes, stirring constantly,
and then serve hot. It should still be green and has a much
better flavour than spinach boiled in the conventional way.

CELERY CABBAGE

1 *celery cabbage*   2 *tablespoons oil*
1 *teaspoon salt*

Celery cabbage is sometimes known as Chinese cabbage. Wash
the cabbage and drain thoroughly. Cut it across the grain into
one-inch slices. Heat a frying pan, add the oil and when hot
cook the cabbage for 2 minutes, stirring constantly. Then add
the salt and cook for 2 more minutes.

Add no water, ample comes from the cabbage to complete
the cooking process. Serve hot.

CELERY

1 *head celery*   1½ *tablespoons oil*
1 *teaspoon salt*   1 *teaspoon sugar*

Wash the celery and cut it diagonally in pieces about an inch
and a half long. Heat a frying pan, add the oil and when hot
put in the celery and cook, stirring, for 2 minutes. Add the salt
and sugar and cook for 1 minute more. Serve hot.

MUSTARD GREENS

2 *lbs. mustard greens*   2 *tablespoons oil*
1 *teaspoon salt*   *little water*

Wash the greens and cut the leaves from the stalks. Cut the stalks into two-inch pieces. Heat a frying pan and add the oil. When hot put in the stalks and cook for 1 minute, stirring. Then add a third of a cup of water and the salt and cook gently for 3 minutes with the cover on. Add the leaves and cook for 2 minutes, stirring constantly. Serve hot.

GREEN CABBAGE

Green cabbage can be cooked in the same way as mustard greens, cooking the thick ends of the leaves first.

SWISS CHARD

Swiss chard is cooked in the same way as mustard greens. First cook the bottom half of the chard, cut into one-inch sections, in the same way as mustard green stalks, adding the top or leafy part of the chard for the last 2 minutes of cooking.

BROCCOLI

1½ *lbs. broccoli*   2 *tablespoons oil*
1 *teaspoon salt*   ¾ *cup water*

Break off the flowerets of broccoli and then peel the big stems
and cut into slices, diagonally, about an inch and a half long.
Wash the broccoli and drain.

Heat a frying pan and add the oil. When it is hot put in the
broccoli and cook, stirring constantly, for 1 minute. Then add
salt and water and cover. Cook gently for 3 minutes. Remove
cover and continue cooking for 5 minutes, stirring frequently.
Serve hot.

ZUCCHINI (SMALL MARROWS)

2 *lbs. zucchini*   2 *tablespoons oil*
2 *tablespoons soy sauce*   1 *teaspoon salt*
dash pepper   ½ *cup water*

Wash the zucchini and slice like a cucumber, about an eighth
of an inch thick. Heat a frying pan and add the oil. When hot
add the zucchini and cook for about 2 minutes. Then add the
salt, pepper and water and cook for a further 5 minutes, still
stirring frequently. Serve hot.

VEGETABLE MARROW

English vegetable marrow can be cooked the same way, but
remove the outer skin if it is tough. Cut into six pieces lengthwise and then slice each piece into slices an eighth of an inch
thick.

Italian squash can also be cooked by the same method.

SPRING ONIONS AND BEAN CURD

2 *bunches spring onions*   1 *pint bean curd*
2 *tablespoons oil*   2 *tablespoons soy sauce*
1 *teaspoon salt*

Slice the bean curd about a quarter of an inch thick. Wash the onions and cut into sections about an inch and a half long. Heat a frying pan and add the oil. When hot put the onions in and cook for 2 minutes, stirring frequently. Then add the bean curd and cook for 2 minutes more, turning frequently but being careful not to break up the bean curd. Lastly add the salt and soy sauce and continue cooking briskly for about a minute. Serve immediately.

PEA PODS

½ *lb. pea pods*   1 *tablespoon oil*
½ *teaspoon salt*   1 *teaspoon soy sauce*

These pea pods, known also as sugar peas, can sometimes be got in Chinatown. They are tender pods in which the peas are just beginning to form. Remove the tops and tails and wash thoroughly. Heat a frying pan and put in the oil. When hot put in the pea pods with whatever water clings to them from the washing. Cook for 1 minute stirring constantly. Then add the salt, soy sauce and 1 tablespoon of water. Cover the pan and cook gently for 3 minutes. Serve hot.

These pea pods are a great addition to any dish of mixed meat and vegetables, whether the meat be chicken, beef or pork. They are very tender and require little cooking. They should still be crisp when served.

They can easily be grown in one's own garden like ordinary peas but be sure to pull the pods before the peas get to be of any size. The latest they should be pulled is when the forming peas make slight bumps along the pod. If not pulled by then they should be left to grow for seed.

BRAISED EGGPLANT

1 *large eggplant*   3 *tablespoons oil*
2 *tablespoons soy sauce*   1 *clove of garlic*
½ *teaspoon salt*   1 *cup water*

Wash the eggplant and cut into four, lengthwise. Then slice
each section in slices about a third of an inch thick. Heat a
frying pan, add the oil and sauté the eggplant slices for 2
minutes, turning frequently. Slice half the garlic clove and
add to the pan with salt, soy sauce and water. Cover the pan
and cook for about 12 to 15 minutes over a low flame. Serve
hot.

SWEET AND SOUR CARROTS

5 *or 6 carrots*   1 *tablespoon oil*
1 *teaspoon salt*
SAUCE:
2 *tablespoons sugar*   1 *tablespoon cornflour*
2 *tablespoons vinegar*   1 *cup water*

Wash the carrots but do not scrape or peel. Cut them
diagonally into slices about three-quarters of an inch thick.
Heat a frying pan and add the oil. When hot sauté the carrot
slices for a full minute. Then add the salt and half a cup of
water and boil the carrots for 4 or 5 minutes, according to their
tenderness. Mix the sugar, vinegar, cornflour and half a cup
of water smoothly and add to the carrots and cook about 2
minutes or until the sauce thickens and becomes translucent.

CELERY SAUTÉ

2 *heads celery*
3 *tablespoons soy sauce*

4 *tablespoons oil*
½ *teaspoon sugar*

Discard the tougher outer stalks of the celery. Break off the other stalks and slice them diagonally half an inch thick. Heat a frying pan, add the oil and when it is smoking hot add the celery and sauté for 3 minutes, stirring constantly. Remove from the flame and stir in the soy sauce and sugar. Return to the fire and cook over a moderate flame for 2 more minutes. Serve immediately.

BAMBOO SHOOTS SAUTÉ

1 *large tin whole bamboo shoots*
¼ *teaspoon salt*

½ *cup oil*
½ *teaspoon sugar*

Cut the bamboo shoots lengthwise a quarter of an inch square so they are like rather slender French fried potatoes. Heat a frying pan, add the oil, then the salt and sugar. When the oil is quite hot add the bamboo shoots and sauté over a brisk flame for about 5 minutes or until they brown slightly. Drain and serve hot.

If it is desired to serve these with sauce, cook the bamboo shoots for 3 minutes then add ¾ cup of chicken stock and cook for 2 minutes more. Remove the bamboo shoots, add 1 teaspoon cornflour mixed in a little water and stir over a moderate flame until the sauce is smooth and thickened. Pour over the bamboo shoots and serve immediately.

MUSHROOMS SAUTÉ

½ lb. good sized mushrooms   3 cups chicken stock
¼ cup oil   4 tablespoons soy sauce
1 teaspoon sugar

Wash the mushrooms and remove the stems, which are not
used in this dish. Cover with boiling water and let stand for 20
minutes. Put the mushrooms, after draining, into a heavy pot
or casserole and cover them with the chicken stock. Cover the
pot and cook in a slow oven (250 degrees) for about 2 hours.

Heat a frying pan and add the oil. When this is hot pour in
the mushrooms and the chicken broth and add the sugar and
soy sauce and cook briskly for about 3 minutes. Serve immediately.

BEAN SPROUT SALAD

1 lb. bean sprouts   ½ cup shredded chicken
DRESSING:
1 tablespoon dry mustard   2 tablespoons vinegar
1 teaspoon sugar   2 tablespoons soy sauce
1 tablespoon sesame oil

Wash the bean sprouts and toss into a saucepan of boiling
water and cook for 4 minutes, reducing the flame to very low
so that the water only just simmers. By this means the sprouts
will be cooked sufficiently but still crisp. Drain them and put
aside to chill.

The best method of making the mustard dressing is to put all
ingredients into a bottle or jar and shake thoroughly until they
are well blended. The sauce should not be freshly made but
allowed to stand some hours before serving.

Arrange the chilled sprouts on a serving dish, top with the
shredded chicken and pour over enough of the dressing to

suit one's taste and serve. The dressing should not be put on until the minute the dish is served, otherwise the sprouts will lose some of their crispness.

SWEET CORN

4 *ears of sweet corn*   1 *small green pepper*
1 *large tomato*   1 *onion*
½ *lb. pork*   4 *tablespoons oil*
4 *tablespoons soy sauce*   1 *teaspoon sherry*
1 *teaspoon salt*

Cut the pork and onion into small cubes and the tomato into fairly small pieces and cut the corn from the ears. (Tinned corn can be used if fresh isn't available.) Parboil the corn. Heat a frying pan and add the oil. When it is hot fry the onion and pork together until the pork is browned. Add the chopped pepper, tomatoes and corn and continue cooking for 3 minutes. Add the sherry, salt and soy sauce and cook for 1 minute more. Serve immediately.

MONKS' FOOD

12 *lotus seeds*	12 *chestnuts*
12 *water chestnuts*	6 *mushrooms*
2 *bamboo shoots*	1 *cup bean sprouts*
1 *cup sliced celery cabbage*	3 *cups chicken stock*
1 *teaspoon salt*	4 *tablespoons soy sauce*
1 *teaspoon cornflour*	2 *tablespoons sherry*
½ *cup diced celery*	4 *tablespoons oil*

Boil the lotus seeds (or almonds if lotus seeds are not available) and the chestnuts for 10 minutes. Remove and drain and peel the chestnuts.

Heat a large frying pan, add the oil and when hot sauté the mushrooms, water chestnuts (quartered), bean sprouts, celery cabbage, bamboo shoots (sliced), lotus seeds and chestnuts for about 5 minutes, turning constantly. Then add the soy sauce, salt, sherry, cornflour and chicken stock. Cover the pan, turn the flame very low and simmer until the vegetables are cooked. Serve hot.

STRING BEANS WITH PORK

1 *lb. string beans*	½ *lb. pork*
1 *clove garlic*	1 *medium onion*
2 *tablespoons oil*	1 *cup chicken stock*
1 *teaspoon chopped ginger*	2 *tablespoons soy sauce*

Heat a frying pan and add the oil. When it is hot fry the garlic and the onion, sliced, until they are a light golden brown. Dice the pork and add to the pan with the ginger. Fry briskly until the pork is well seared, about 4 minutes. Remove from the fire and stir in the soy sauce and add the string beans, each one cut in two or left whole if they are small. Add the chicken stock and simmer the whole gently for 5 minutes. Serve immediately.

BRAISED BAMBOO SHOOTS

1 *large tin bamboo shoots*	1 *teaspoon sugar*
½ *teaspoon salt*	2 *tablespoons soy sauce*
1 *tablespoon sherry*	¼ *cup chicken stock*
¼ *cup oil*	

A large tin of bamboo shoots usually contains four. Slice them lengthwise so they are like French fried potatoes but about a quarter of an inch square. Dry them in a cloth.

Heat a sauté pan and add the oil. When hot add the salt, sugar, soy sauce, sherry and chicken stock. Add the sliced bamboo shoots and cook over a brisk flame for about ten minutes. Serve hot.

Always serve the Chinese pepper and salt mixture with this dish so that the bamboo shoots can be dipped in it before eating.

FRIED SPINACH

1 *lb. spinach*	1 *bamboo shoot*
8 *mushrooms*	1 *teaspoon salt*
¼ *cup chicken stock*	¼ *cup oil*

Wash the spinach well and cut it in two-inch lengths. Heat a frying pan and add the oil. When hot add the salt and then the spinach and fry for 2 minutes. Then add the stock and the mushrooms and bamboo shoot sliced. Fry all together for 3 more minutes and serve hot.

VEGETABLE OMELETTE

1 *onion*	5 *eggs*
1 *green pepper*	3 *pieces celery*
4 *mushrooms*	1 *teaspoon salt*
3 *tablespoons oil*	*dash pepper*

Chop the onion fairly small, slice the mushrooms and cut the pepper into inch squares. Dice the celery.

Heat a frying pan and add the oil. When hot fry the onion a golden brown then add the other vegetables and cook for about 15 seconds. Remove and drain. Beat the eggs lightly and add to the vegetables, mixing thoroughly.

Return about 1 tablespoon of oil to the pan and when it is fairly hot pour in the egg and vegetable mixture. Reduce the heat and cook slowly until the omelette is set. Cut into pieces about two inches square and serve immediately.

In China as elsewhere there are a dozen ways of cooking rice, indeed there are as many ways as there are of mixing martinis and the advocates of each method will defend that method to the death as the *only* possible method. Here are four methods of making boiled rice. The second is a Cantonese method and the third I have found easiest and invariably satisfactory.

1. Wash the rice in cold water several times until the water pours off clear. Then add two cups of water to each cup of rice, putting it in a large saucepan with a cover. Boil it over a hot flame until the water is evaporated and do not stir while boiling. Then set the saucepan on the side of the stove (or in a cool oven), leaving the cover on while the rice absorbs all moisture left in the pot.

2. Wash the rice thoroughly in cold water. Put it in a pottery vessel like an earthenware casserole with a cover. Pour water in until it reaches one finger joint above the rice. Bring to a boil over a hot fire and then turn the flame as low as possible. Put the lid on and when the water is completely absorbed the rice will be done. This makes very beautiful flaky rice. True, there is a crusty bit in the bottom of the cooking vessel but advocates of this method consider the perfection of the rice well worth the cleaning out job that has to follow.

3. Wash the rice thoroughly under the cold tap. Fill a large saucepan half full of water, bring to the boil and add exactly one teaspoon of vinegar. Throw the rice into the boiling water and keep it boiling, uncovered, for 15 to 18 minutes. Remove from the fire and pour the contents of the saucepan into a large fine meshed sieve. Hold the sieve under the hot tap and thoroughly rinse the rice. All the grains will separate.

Put the rice in the top of a double boiler if it is not required immediately. When needed it can easily be heated again.

4. Wash the rice thoroughly in five or six changes of water, rubbing it between the palms. Then in a large saucepan put rice and cold water in the proportion of one cup of rice to $1\frac{1}{2}$ cups of water. Place over a moderate flame and bring to a roaring boil, keeping the cover on. When the steam begins to escape turn the flame low and cook for about 20 minutes by which time the water should be absorbed and the rice fluffy. Keep the saucepan over a tiny flame or at the side of the stove until ready to use.

FRIED RICE

3 *cups cooked rice*
2 *eggs*
$\frac{1}{2}$ *teaspoon salt*
$\frac{1}{4}$ *cup chopped shrimp*
2 *tablespoons oil*

1 *large onion*
1 *tablespoon soy sauce*
$\frac{1}{2}$ *cup chopped ham*
1 *small bamboo shoot chopped*

Heat a large iron frying pan, add the oil and fry the chopped onion until brown. Then add the ham, shrimp and bamboo shoot. Add the cold rice and sauté until the whole begins to brown, turning over occasionally. When the whole mixture is hot add the beaten eggs, stirring all the time, the soy sauce and the salt. Add more soy if taste suggests it.

Fried rice is really a means of using up left-overs, but over the years has established itself as a prime dish in Chinese cookery and nowadays no Chinese meal seems complete without it. It is, I believe, Cantonese in origin but so good is it that it has achieved universal recognition.

What gives the dish its basic quality is the combination of rice, soy sauce and onion fried together. After that it can be given almost any left over—bacon, ham, shrimp, mushrooms, bamboo shoot. Any one of them will do or bits of all of them may go in and an egg always adds to the flavour. The egg can be beaten and added, or it can be stirred to mix yolk and white then fried and cut into strips before being added to the rice mixture. Care should always be taken not to make it too rich with oil. When served it should be a reasonably dry dish.

FRIED RICE WITH CRAB MEAT I

4 cups cooked rice
½ cup chopped onion
4 tablespoons peanut oil
pepper and salt

2 cups crab meat
2 eggs, beaten
4 tablespoons soy sauce

Put the oil into a hot shallow pan and sauté the crab meat slightly. Add the onion and when it is half cooked add the other ingredients and fry for 3 or 4 minutes.

FRIED RICE WITH CRAB MEAT II

2 cups crab meat
1 onion
4 tablespoons oil
2 teaspoons salt

4 cups cooked rice
3 eggs
3 tablespoons soy sauce
dash of pepper

Heat a shallow pan, add the oil and when hot fry the onion, sliced, until it begins to brown. Then add the crab meat, shredded or in small pieces, and sauté for 2 minutes. Add the cooked rice and continue cooking until the rice is hot. Beat the eggs and pour slowly over the rice, stirring constantly. The egg should shred as it cooks and be mixed thoroughly in. Finally add the salt, soy sauce and pepper, continue cooking for a minute and serve immediately.

FRIED RICE AND SHRIMP

2 cups cooked rice
½ cup sliced onion
2 eggs beaten
3 tablespoons peanut oil

1 lb. cooked shrimps
½ cup sliced mushrooms
2 tablespoons soy sauce
salt to taste

Put the oil into a hot shallow pan and cook the onion until it begins to brown. Add the shrimp and cook for a minute. Then add mushrooms, soy sauce and salt and cook for a couple of minutes. Add the cooked rice, stirring all ingredients together. Lastly add the beaten eggs and fry all together until the eggs are cooked, which should be about a minute or so.

BEEF AND RICE

½ lb. beef cubed
2 small onions sliced
2 tablespoons soy sauce
salt to taste

4 cups cooked rice
1 sweet pepper sliced
2 tablespoons oil

Put the oil in a hot frying pan and sauté the beef, onion and pepper for a minute. Add the soy sauce and cook gently for 2 minutes. Make a bed of hot cooked rice on a dish and pour over it the contents of the pan and serve at once.

An alternative is to use pork instead of beef.

CRISP RICE

Some methods of cooking rice or re-heating rice leave a crusty quantity of rice in the bottom of the saucepan or casserole. Break these out in fairly large pieces, put them a few at a time in a wire basket and dip into very hot fat, frying until they are a crisp golden brown, drain cool and serve as an hors d'oeuvre.

These can also be made from left-over glutinous rice. Form the sticky rice into flat lumps and fry as above.

Crisp rice can also be served hot.

DESSERTS

ALMOND TEA

1 *cup fine ground almonds*
4 *tablespoons cornflour*
1 *cup chopped blanched*
    walnuts

8 *cups water*
1 *tin evaporated milk*
    (*unsweetened*)
1 *cup sugar*

This is really misnamed. It is not tea but a popular Chinese dessert about the consistency of hot custard. Mix the ground almonds (they must be very fine so that the result is very smooth), the sugar, cornflour and 1 cup of water to make a smooth thick paste. Then slowly add the rest of the water and the tin of milk. Cook the whole in a double boiler until it thickens. Add the finely chopped walnuts, cook for 2 minutes more and serve hot in Chinese tea cups.

FRIED WALNUTS

1½ *cups shelled walnuts*
½ *cup oil*

½ *cup sugar*

Blanch the walnuts and pour one cup of hot water over them and let them stand for 2 minutes. Drain and mix them with the sugar (fine granulated). Let them remain overnight or at least from morning until evening. They should then be dry.

Heat a frying pan, add the oil and fry the walnuts until they are brown. If you prefer, use more oil and fry them in a wire basket so they are easily lifted out when done. Serve either hot or cold.

WALNUT AND DATE TEA

1 *cup blanched walnuts*   ½ *cup rice*
½ *cup sugar*   12 *dates*

This again is misnamed a tea. Boil the dates in a little water for
5 minutes and then put them through a sieve. Wash the rice
thoroughly and soak in water for 10 minutes. Grind the walnuts
and rice together and add enough of the rice water to make a
smooth paste. To this add the sugar, the date paste and 3 cups
of water. Put the mixture in a saucepan and stir constantly
until it boils. Boil for 10 seconds, still stirring. It should then
be thickened. Serve hot in Chinese tea cups.

EIGHT PRECIOUS PUDDING

1½ *cups glutinous rice*   ½ *cup sugar*
12 *dates*   16 *candied lotus seeds*
6 *preserved green plums*   ¼ *lb. blanched walnuts*
36 *raisins*   12 *water melon seeds, shelled*
6 *maraschino cherries*   12 *dragon eye nuts*
SAUCE:
½ *cup sugar*, 1 *tablespoon cornflour and* 1 *cup water boiled together
    for 5 minutes*

Wash the rice and cook in 6 cups of water until soft. Drain and
add ½ cup sugar. Rub a bowl with butter and arrange the fruit
on the bottom in any pattern that pleases. Place the cooked rice
on top of the arranged fruits without disturbing the pattern.
Steam for 45 minutes. Turn upside down on a dish, pour the
hot sauce over and serve.

This can be made with any preserved fruits desired and if
dragon nuts aren't available almonds can be substituted.

G

CANDIED DATES

½ lb. large dates   1 cup sugar
¾ cup cold water   ⅛ teaspoon cream of tartar

Place each date (stoned) on an orange stick. Mix the sugar and cream of tartar and cook with the water until the syrup will thread when dropped from the end of a spoon. Remove from the fire and dip each date until thoroughly covered with syrup. Allow to cool and harden.

Walnuts can be treated the same way.

ORANGE TEA

2 large oranges   1 cup sugar
3 cups water   ½ cup glutinous flour

Cut the oranges in half and with a small spoon scoop out the pulp and juice and stand it to one side. Mix the glutinous flour with a little cold water until it forms a stiff paste. Roll it into small balls. Boil the sugar and water together and drop in the flour balls. Continue to boil until they float, when they will be done. Add the orange pulp and juice and boil for 5 seconds. Serve hot in Chinese tea cups.

GRAPE AND ORANGE TEA

Proceed exactly as for Orange Tea but when adding the orange pulp add also half a pound of grapes, peeled and stoned.

LOTUS SEED TEA

1 cup lotus seeds
7 cups hot water

½ cup sugar
2 tablespoons cornflour

Wash the lotus seeds, which are something like filbert nuts, and add two cups of hot water to cover. Boil for 5 minutes. Pour off the water and add two cups of fresh hot water and boil for another 10 minutes. Skin the nuts and with a pointed knife remove the green part of the nut. Put the nuts in a bowl and add a cup of hot water and steam for 20 minutes. Add two cups of water and the sugar and bring to a boil. Add the cornflour and stir. Add a few slices of preserved cherry, cook till the cornflour thickens and serve hot.

DATE CAKES

2 cups dates
½ cup walnut meats
⅓ cup sugar
1 tablespoon butter

1 cup glutinous flour
tablespoon sesame seeds
1 cup water

Wash the dates and bring to the boil in a cup of water. Then simmer until the water disappears. Skin the dates and pass through a sieve until you have a cup of pulp. Add the butter and glutinous flour and knead well. Make small balls of this mixture and then flatten out thinly.

Fry the sesame seeds in a little oil for 2 seconds and add to them the walnut meats, chopped finely, and the sugar. Put a teaspoon of this filling on each piece of flattened dough and enclose in a ball. Roll them lightly in flour and steam for 15 minutes. Serve hot.

Before steaming these date balls can be lightly pressed into wooden moulds to give them a design. The Chinese, in steaming them, put each ball on a piece of bamboo leaf and they are served still resting on the leaf.

ALMOND MOULD

1 *cup fine ground almonds*   1 *tablespoon powdered gelatine*
sugar to taste

Boil the ground almonds in two cups of water to extract as much flavour as possible and strain through a cloth. If the resulting almond water has insufficient flavour add a touch of almond extract. Put the water in a saucepan, heat and add the gelatine powder, stirring until it is dissolved. Put in shallow flat bottomed dish and chill until it sets like jelly. Cut this into various interesting shapes and put several pieces into Chinese tea cups half-filled with cold sweetened water. Serve cold.

WALNUT TEA

½ *lb. walnut meats*   ⅔ *cup rice flour*
4 *cups water*   ⅓ *cup brown sugar*

Grind the walnuts until they are very fine and add to three cups of boiling water and cook for half an hour. Strain through a cloth and discard the walnut meat. To the walnut flavoured water add the sugar and rice flour and mix until smooth. Add another cup of water and, stirring constantly, bring to a boil and cook for 3 or 4 minutes. Serve hot in Chinese tea cups.

NEW YEAR DUMPLINGS I

These are boiled, stuffed dumplings and although called New
Year Dumplings are usually not served until the Chinese moon
year is fifteen days old, that is when the first moon of the year
becomes full. They are served at dinner but also eaten as a
between-meals snack or just before going to bed to stave off any
hunger pangs that might appear during the night. Make the
stuffing first.

STUFFING:

2 ozs. ground almonds	a few watermelon seed kernels
2 ozs. ground walnuts	if available
2 ozs. sesame seed, roasted and	½ cup sugar
then crushed	1 tablespoon oil

COVERING:

1 lb. of glutinous rice flour

Mix the stuffing ingredients thoroughly together and then take
a teaspoon at a time and roll into a ball about half an inch in
diameter. Then take a serving tray and spread on the bottom
some of the rice flour. Damp the stuffing balls and put them
on the tray. Lift it in both hands and with a circular motion
keep rolling the balls round so that they all get coated with the
flour. When they reach the stage where they are too dry to
gather more flour, sprinkle or spray them with a little more
water and go on with the process. Try and make all the flour
adhere to the balls.

Fill a large saucepan ⅔ full of water and bring it to a boil.
Drop the balls in and boil for 5 minutes, when the dumplings
will float to the surface. Then pour a cupful of very cold water
in, bring to the boil once more and boil for another 3 minutes.
They can be served either hot or cold.

NEW YEAR DUMPLINGS II

1 *lb. granulated sugar*   1 *lb. sesame cakes*
1 *lb. walnut meats blanched* ½ *cup oil*
1½ *lbs. glutinous rice flour*

If sesame cakes are not available from a Chinese food shop, crushed macaroons can be used with a little sesame seed added. Crush the walnuts finely and add 4 tablespoons of sugar. Roll the sesame cakes as finely as possible. Add the rest of sugar to the oil and blend well and stir in the crushed sesame cakes. Knead it thoroughly and then roll into balls the size of a large cherry. Flatten these and put some of the sugar and walnut mixture in and roll into balls again. Make them as round as possible and put aside to harden.

Add cold water slowly to the rice flour until it is about the consistency of pastry dough. Roll it out fairly thinly and cut into pieces big enough to wrap round the prepared fillings. See the filling is completely sealed in and drop them four or five at a time into a saucepan of boiling water. Stir the water so they do not stick to the bottom. When they rise to the top keep cooking for 3 or 4 minutes more. When all are cooked, sweeten the water in which they were boiled. Half fill small serving bowls with this sweetened water, add three of the dumplings to each bowl and serve hot.

LYCHEES

The Chinese like a little fruit at the end of their banquets and, in their season, enjoy peaches, pears and persimmon in the north and mango, pumelo and the incomparable lychee in the south.

Fresh lychees are imported into England from South Africa and can also be obtained tinned and dried. In the dried version the large juicy fruit is dehydrated until it is the size of a large raisin, and is good eating. The tinned version is nothing like the fresh lychee but it is still a delicious fruit and either version gives an authentic Chinese touch to the end of a meal.

ICE CREAM

In quite recent years ice cream has become a popular dessert among Chinese, though a Chinese epicure of the old school would be horrified by its production at a banquet. However it makes quite a good ending to a Chinese meal and a simple water ice is even better.

LOTUS SEED TEA

1 *cup preserved lotus seeds*   ¼ *cup sugar*
1 *tablespoon cornflour*   3 *cups water*

Use candied lotus seeds if obtainable, if not increase the quantity of sugar a little. Mix the cornflour, sugar and water together and bring to the boil. Continue boiling for 2 minutes then add the lotus seeds, turn the flame down and simmer for 1 minute. Serve hot.

TANGERINE TEA

5 *tangerines*   ½ *cup sugar*
3 *cups water*   3 *tablespoons glutinous rice*
                                  flour

Peel the tangerines and remove skin and seeds from the
sections leaving only the pulp. Mix together sugar, flour and
water and bring to a boil. After it has boiled 5 seconds (during
which stir constantly) add the tangerine pulp, turn down the
flame and simmer for 2 minutes. Serve hot immediately.

ORANGE AND PINEAPPLE TEA

3 *large oranges*   1 *slice tinned pineapple or* 4 *or*
¾ *cup sugar*   5 *chunks*
4 *tablespoons glutinous flour*   3 *cups water*

Keep only the pulp of the oranges as in the previous recipe.
Mix the flour with enough cold water to make a paste and
form this into tiny balls like marbles. Boil together the sugar
and water, add the paste balls and boil until they float. Then
add the orange pulp and the pineapple shredded. Simmer for
30 seconds and serve hot.

GREEN PEA CAKE

½ *lb. split green peas*   ¾ *cup sugar*
2 *cups water*   2 *tablespoons cornflour*

Soak the peas until they swell to normal size then simmer them
in the water until they break apart. Put them through a fine
sieve and return to the saucepan. Add the sugar and the cornflour mixed with a little water. Stir the whole mixture
thoroughly while bringing to the boil. Pour into a shallow tray
and cool until set, in the refrigerator if possible. Cut the mass
into one-inch cubes and serve.

GREEN PEA PUDDING

½ *lb. split green peas*   ½ *cup sugar*
2 *cups water*   2 *tablespoons oil*

This is a variation of the above served hot. It comes from
Szechuen province. Soak the peas in water until they expand
and then simmer gently in the water until they break up. Pass
through a fine sieve and add the sugar to the purée. Heat a pan
and add the oil. When it is hot pour in the purée. Stir to
prevent burning and cook over a low flame until thoroughly
hot. Serve immediately.

STEAMED DATE CAKE

¾ *lb. dates*   ½ *lb. glutinous rice flour*

Boil the dates for 5 minutes in plain water. Remove all skin and
the stones. Knead the date purée with the rice flour and the
resulting paste should be fairly stiff. Flatten out the paste until
it is about half an inch thick. Then cut it into rounds about the
size of small macaroons.

The Chinese make a thin bed of bamboo leaves on which to
place these for steaming, but the washed leaves of rushes will
do equally well. Place the leaves on a rack which will go in an
asparagus cooker over an inch of hot water. Get the water
boiling fiercely and steam the cakes for about 5 minutes. Serve
the cakes hot. They will be fairly soft but should keep their
shape.

ALMOND JUNKET

1 *cup ground almonds*   3 *cups water*
4 *tablespoons sugar*   1 *tablespoon powdered gelatine*

Add the ground almonds to the water and boil for 5 minutes.
Strain, discarding the almonds. To the almond milk remaining
add the sugar and the gelatine, stirring over a low flame until
the gelatine is dissolved. Cool until it forms a jelly, which is
then cut into cubes and served in rice bowls or tea cups in cold
sweetened water.

ALMOND CAKES

1½ cups wheat flour
½ cup oil
1 egg
saltspoon almond extract

½ teaspoon baking powder
¾ cup sugar
¼ cup ground almonds

Sift the flour into a bowl with the baking powder and then add
the oil slowly. This can be either peanut or sesame oil. Then
add the ground almonds, almond extract and the sugar. Add
the egg without beating. If too stiff a dough, add a little water
but be sure the dough is not too soft. Form the dough into
balls and then press down into biscuit shape so they are about
half an inch thick and not less than two inches in diameter.
Press one whole blanched almond into the top of each cake
and bake in a moderate oven for about 12 to 15 minutes, when
they should be a light golden brown.

PEKING GRIDDLE CAKES

2 cups flour	1 tablespoon oil
small onion	1 tablespoon chopped shrimp
1½ teaspoons salt	⅔ cup water

Add the water (not too cold) to the flour and knead well. Add another spoonful of water and knead again. Roll the dough out a quarter of an inch thick and brush the oil over the surface. Then spread over it a mixture of the salt, chopped onion and chopped shrimp. Roll it up like a Swiss roll and cut into slices about an inch thick. Twist the ends to enclose the filling and then flatten out with a rolling pin so that the pieces are about a third of an inch thick. Put them on a hot griddle or the top of the stove, without grease of any kind, and cook until both sides are brown. Serve hot.

STEAMED BREAD (MAN T'OU)

3 cups flour	4 teaspoons baking powder
1 cup water	

Mix the baking powder into the flour thoroughly and then add the water slowly. Knead the dough well and then leave for 2 hours to allow it to rise. Knead it again lightly, cut into pieces and shape like buns. Rub with flour lightly and steam for 20 minutes.

CORNMEAL BREAD

1 cup flour
2 teaspoons baking powder
½ cup water

1 cup cornmeal
½ cup sugar

Sift the flour and then mix in the baking powder. Next mix in the cornmeal and then the sugar. Add the water and mix well. Shape into buns and steam for 20 minutes.

STEAMED YEAST BREAD

2½ cups flour
½ cake yeast

2 cups water
½ teaspoon salt

Make the water lukewarm and soak the yeast in it. When the yeast is soft work water and yeast into the flour. Knead it well and put into a warm place to rise until it is four times its original size. Knead it again, using a little flour to prevent it getting sticky.

Divide the dough into a dozen pieces and work each piece into a round dumpling. Let them rise for 6 or 7 minutes and then steam them for 15 to 20 minutes.

'PEKING DOILIES' OR PAO PING

5 *cups flour*
1 *teaspoon salt*

2 *cups boiling water*
¼ *cup oil*

These are the paper thin pancakes in which Peking Duck (page 53) is wrapped before eating but they can be used with various fillings, one of which is given below.

Add the salt to the flour and sift. Then pour in the boiling water, stirring the while. When all the water is added transfer to a board and knead carefully. It should make a fairly stiff dough. Roll it out a quarter of an inch thick and cut out pieces with a two-inch biscuit cutter. These are then rolled out as thin as possible and as round as possible. A good method of getting them thin is to flour two such pieces, put one on top of the other and roll out together as thin as possible. Then separate the two and you have paper thin doilies.

Smear each finished doily with a little oil and dust with flour lightly. Use the minimum of oil. Place them on a griddle to cook and turn often to avoid burning.

FILLING:

2 *eggs, beaten*
2 *ozs. each of cooked sliced roast duck, ham, cold chicken and roast pork*
Hiosin or thick soy sauce

½ *cup bean sprouts*
¼ *lb. spinach*
1 *cup sliced celery cabbage*
1 *cucumber, sliced*
1 *spring onion top*

Fry the beaten eggs and slice thinly. Put them with the various sliced cold meats on a large plate and place in the centre of the table. Boil the vegetables for about 5 minutes with a little salt in the water. Place each one on a separate plate and arrange these round the dish of meat. Have two plates of warm doilies on the table and two plates of the soy paste.

Place a doily in the palm of the left hand, add a little of the soy paste and then put on the pancake whatever meats and vegetables you fancy. Roll up the pancake and eat. As you can see, dozens of variations of content are possible. It is a perfect way of using up all sorts of left-overs.

MEAT DUMPLINGS (CHIAO TZU)

1 *lb. spinach*	1 *lb. lean pork*
1 *onion*	1 *tablespoon chopped ginger*
4 *tablespoons oil*	3 *tablespoons soy sauce*
1 *tablespoon salt*	3 *cups flour*

This is one of the favourite dishes of north China and at a family meal often provides the principal dish for the evening meal.

Boil the spinach for 3 minutes and put it in a cloth to squeeze out all water possible. Make a fairly stiff dough of the flour and cold water. Knead it well and roll it out about an inch thick. Cut it into small pieces and roll out very thin and round. When rolled the pieces should be about 2½ inches in diameter.

Heat a frying pan, add the oil and when hot sauté the onion, finely chopped, the ginger and the pork, finely chopped or put through the mincer. Add the soy sauce and salt. Remove from the fire and when cool add it to the cooked spinach. This dish is improved if the 4 tablespoons of oil is equal quantities of peanut and sesame oil.

Put a good spoonful of the pork and spinach mixture on each little pancake and fold over and pinch the edges together so that the shape is a half-moon. Bring half a saucepan of water to a strong boil and drop the dumplings in about three at a time and cook for 3 minutes. Alternatively they can be steamed, but then need longer cooking. Serve hot.

If any are left over they can be fried the following day until they are lightly brown, and served hot.

The thinner the dough is rolled out the better. This dish has been known in China for centuries and the Chinese believe that Marco Polo took the recipe back to Italy and that from it Italian ravioli developed.

FRIED MEAT DUMPLINGS

2 cups flour	¾ cup boiling water

FILLING:

1 cup finely chopped pork	2 tablespoons oil
1 tablespoon finely chopped onion	1 teaspoon salt
	2 tablespoons soy sauce
½ cup chopped bamboo shoots	1 tablespoon sherry

This is a variation of *chiao tzu* and just as popular. Mix all the filling ingredients together. Mix the flour and water in a bowl and knead into a fairly stiff dough. Cut the dough into small pieces as in the previous recipe. (If you prefer, roll the dough out in large pieces but very thin and cut with a round biscuit cutter.) On each circle of dough put a teaspoonful of the mixture, cover with another circle and pinch the edges together to seal in the filling.

Heat a frying pan, add oil generously and when it is hot fry the dumplings a few at a time until they are golden brown on both sides. Serve hot.

SPRING ROLLS

2½ cups flour	1 cup boiling water
1 teaspoon salt	⅛ cup oil
	enough oil for deep frying

FILLING:

6 mushrooms	2 stalks celery
½ lb. bean sprouts	½ lb. shredded pork
1 tablespoon soy sauce	½ tablespoon sherry
1 teaspoon salt	3 tablespoons soy sauce
3 tablespoons oil	2 teaspoons cornflour

Make what are known as 'Peking doilies' (page 204) from the first ingredients. Add the salt to the flour then pour the boiling water in slowly. Knead it well and cut into pieces which when rolled out as thin as possible are roughly rectangular and about four inches by six. Lightly brush the surface with oil and dust with flour. Heat a large frying pan or griddle and, without oil, cook the pancakes till they are faintly brown but on no account burnt.

To prepare the filling cut the celery (or bamboo shoot if you prefer) and put it with the bean sprouts into 2 tablespoons of hot oil and sauté lightly. Remove and put in a dish. Reheat the pan and sauté the mushrooms, finely sliced, and the pork which should be mixed with 1 tablespoon soy sauce, the sherry and 1 teaspoon of salt. The pork should be cooked about half a minute and then added to the vegetables previously cooked. Mix well and allow to cool.

Then spread about 1½ tablespoons of the mixture evenly over each doily. Fold the sides in and roll up like a Swiss roll. Seal each edge with a mixture of cornflour and water. When this has dried and the rolls are sealed fry them in deep fat until they are golden brown. Serve hot.

CANTONESE EGG ROLL

½ cup cooked pork
2 teaspoons salt
1 teaspoon sugar
1 small carrot
2 eggs
1 cup oil

½ cup cooked shrimps
2 tablespoons oil
1 spring onion finely chopped
1 piece celery
½ cup flour

Beat 1½ eggs, half cup of water and ½ teaspoon of salt together and then beat it into the flour to make a very thin batter. Brush the bottom of a frying pan with a little oil and pour in enough batter to make a very thin pancake. Cook over moderate flame for 1 minute and do not turn over. Lay the pancake aside to cool. Continue making very thin pancakes until all the batter is used.

Shred enough carrot to make 1 tablespoon, and celery the same. Cook in boiling water for 5 minutes then drain and cool. Chop the onion finely and put the pork through a mincer. Add to the onion and the pork 1 teaspoon salt, the shrimp (chopped), 2 teaspoons of oil, the sugar and a dash of pepper. Mix this thoroughly together and place a heaping tablespoonful on each pancake. Spread it out, turn the edges in and roll up like a Swiss roll. Seal the end with the remaining egg slightly beaten. Leave to dry so that the filling is well sealed in.

Put 1 cup of oil in a deep frying pan and when it is very hot drop in the rolls and cook until they are golden brown. Remove, drain and serve hot.

NOODLES

EGG NOODLES

4 *eggs*	2 *cups flour*
1 *tablespoon cornflour*	½ *teaspoon salt*

Mix the eggs into the flour without beating them and then add the salt. Make into a smooth dough. Dust a little cornflour on to the pastryboard and roll out the dough as thin as possible and then dust it with cornflour. Roll the whole thing round the rolling pin and press it with the palms of the hands. Roll the dough out flat again and repeat the whole process four times, then fold neatly on the pastry board and cut into thin strips.

DRAWN NOODLES

If you wish to try to make drawn noodles you may be amused fascinated or exasperated. There used to be restaurants in Peking where the noodle maker came to the table with a lump of dough and drew them out beautifully before your eyes in a matter of two or three minutes. They were then tossed into a pot and served steaming hot a few minutes later.

For drawn noodles make the dough as described above but instead of rolling out thinly make it into a roll of dough about two inches in diameter. Have a pastry board handy with a thick dusting of flour on it. Take the roll of dough by the ends and draw it out as far as the arms will comfortably go, say about four feet. Then double it over so the ends are together in the left hand and grasp what was the middle in the right hand. Once more draw out to four feet, after rolling the middle in the

flour on the board. The number of strands obviously doubles
each time this is done, two, four, eight, sixteen, thirty-two.
Keep the process going as long as possible until the strands
are very thin. Then cut off the two ends, and, if you have been
lucky, you will have sixty-four noodles almost four feet long.

It isn't easy at first but it is an art that can be learned and the
results are good. Noodles made this way have a totally different
texture.

To cook them drop into boiling water and boil briskly for
10 minutes. Then rinse them in cold water or under the cold
tap and put in a double boiler to keep warm for serving.

PLAIN NOODLES

3 *eggs*   2½ *cups flour*

Yet another system of making noodles is to beat the three eggs
lightly and then mix them into the flour. Knead into a soft
dough, cover with a damp cloth and leave for 10 minutes.
Then knead again for 5 minutes and sprinkle the dough with
cornflour.

Take a large pastry board and roll out the dough very thinly,
about 20 inches wide. Fold this neatly into pleats leaving an
inch unfolded. Cut across the pleats with a sharp knife, each
cut about the thickness of a rasher of bacon. Hold up by that
unfolded inch and shake out the noodles. Drop them into
boiling water and, if they are very thin, cook for 5 minutes
(longer if they are thicker). Hold them a minute under the cold
tap to separate them and put in the top of a double boiler
ready for serving. Or, if they are to be fried, put them on one
side to cool.

FRIED NOODLES

½ lb. noodles
½ lb. bean sprouts or string
  beans
4 mushrooms, sliced
¼ lb. pork or chicken, sliced

2 eggs
1 bamboo shoot, sliced
2 stalks celery, cut in 1 inch
  lengths
½ cup oil

SAUCE:
5 tablespoons soy sauce
1 tablespoon cornflour

2 teaspoons salt

Brush the bottom of a small hot frying pan with oil and add the beaten eggs one at a time. Cook each one for a minute so that it forms a thin pancake. Put on one side to cool, then slice into strips like noodles.

Cook the noodles in boiling water, or else take cold, previously boiled noodles. Smear the meat with the sauce mixture, heat a frying pan and add 4 tablespoons oil. Sauté the meat and then add the sliced vegetables and cook for 10 seconds. Remove them from the pan.

Reheat the pan and add 6 tablespoons of oil and when it is hot fry the noodles for 10 seconds if they are freshly boiled or double that time if they are cold. Add the meat and vegetables to the pan and cook a few seconds, stirring. Transfer all to a warm serving dish and decorate the top of the noodles with the sliced fried eggs. A little shredded ham on top of the egg adds to both appearance and flavour.

NOODLES WITH CHICKEN SAUCE

fresh noodles   *chicken stock with cornflour*
salt to taste

Boil freshly made noodles until they are tender. Then take a
deep frying pan and heat. Smear the bottom with oil and to
1 lb. of noodles placed in the pan add a cup of rich chicken
stock to which 2 teaspoons cornflour have been added. Cook over
a moderate flame until the sauce thickens a little and becomes
translucent. Serve hot immediately.

YANGCHOW NOODLES

noodles, freshly made or   *½ lb. lean pork*
*   bought*   *½ cup chicken stock*
½ cup tinned mushrooms or 3   *2 stalks celery*
*   fresh ones*   *2 tablespoons oil*
2 spring onions or 1 onion   *1 tablespoon cornflour*
1 teaspoon salt   *1 teaspoon soy sauce*

Cut the pork into thin slices and sauté in a frying pan to which
2 tablespoons of oil and 1 teaspoon of salt have been added.
When the meat is brown add the celery and onions cut in half-
inch lengths and cook all together for 5 minutes, stirring constantly. Then add the chicken stock, turn the flame low and
cook for 5 minutes. Uncover the pan and add the mushrooms,
sliced. Blend together the cornflour, soy sauce and a little
water. Cook until the sauce thickens, stirring frequently.

Boil the noodles in salted water for 5 minutes, rinse for a
minute under the cold tap and then keep them warm in a
double boiler. Fill individual serving bowls with the noodles
and place on top the meat and vegetable mixture.

NOODLES WITH HAM SAUCE

boiled noodles
1 *cup beef or chicken stock*
1 *teaspoon cornflour*
2 *tablespoons oil*

1 *cup chopped ham*
2 *stalks celery*
1 *small onion*
1 *egg*

After boiling the noodles, place them in a serving dish and keep warm. Heat a frying pan and add 2 tablespoons oil. When hot add the chopped ham and the celery and onion, diced. Cook over a moderate flame for 5 minutes and then add the stock. Cover the pan, lower the flame and cook 3 minutes more. Mix the cornflour and the slightly beaten egg with $\frac{1}{4}$ cup of water and add this to the ham and vegetables. Cook over moderate flame until the sauce thickens, then pour over the noodles and serve immediately.

FRIED NOODLES

2 *cups egg noodles*   1 *pint oil*

Boil the egg noodles in salted water until they are quite tender. Drain them and rinse with cold water. Allow to get quite cold.

Add the oil to a deep fryer and bring it to not less than 375 degrees. Using a wire basket, put a quarter of the noodles in it, lower into the boiling oil and cook until they are golden brown. Remove, drain and keep hot until the rest of the noodles are similarly cooked. Serve hot.

EGG NOODLES

2 *cups wheat flour*   4 *eggs*
1 *tablespoon cornflour*   ½ *teaspoon salt*

Sift the flour into a bowl and add the salt. Mix in the four eggs without beating them. If they make the dough a little wet, add a little more flour.

Dust a pastry board with the cornflour and roll out the dough as thin as possible. Aim at paper thinness. Then dust the top of the rolled-out dough with more cornflour and roll the dough round the rolling pin. Press the dough to the pin with the palms then remove it and roll the dough flat once more and again as thin as possible. Repeat twice and finally fold the rolled-out sheet three or four times and cut the width the noodles are required with a sharp knife. Shake the noodles out and drop into boiling salted water.

BOILED NOODLES WITH HAM SAUCE

2 *cups noodles*   1 *cup shredded ham*
1 *egg*   4 *tablespoons chopped celery*
1 *onion*   ½ *clove garlic*
1 *cup beef stock*   1 *tablespoon cornflour*
½ *teaspoon salt*   3 *tablespoons oil*

Cook the noodles in boiling salted water until tender, drain, rinse quickly in cold water and place in a warm serving dish.

Heat a frying pan, add the oil and when hot add the shredded ham (put through a mincer if you like), the celery, sliced onion and chopped garlic. Cook over a moderate flame for 4 minutes then add the beef stock and continue cooking for 4 more minutes. Mix together the cornflour, the egg, lightly beaten, and about 2 tablespoons of water. When thoroughly mixed pour this into the pan and continue cooking until it thickens, stirring constantly. Pour over the noodles and serve immediately.

FRIED NOODLES WITH CHICKEN
LIVERS

2 cups egg noodles
1 small onion
1 cup chicken stock
pepper to taste
SAUCE:
2 tablespoons cornflour
1 tablespoon soy sauce

¾ lb. chicken livers
2 tablespoons chopped celery
1 teaspoon salt
4 tablespoons oil

2 tablespoons water

Cook the noodles in boiling salted water until done, drain them, rinse in cold water and put aside to cool, if possible in a refrigerator.

Cut each chicken liver into two or three pieces and slice the onion.

Heat a frying pan, add the oil and when hot arrange the noodles in it like a very thick pancake. Fry until brown on the under side then turn and brown the other side. When done, put aside in a warm serving dish.

If necessary add a little more oil to the pan and when hot fry the onion until it begins to brown then add the livers and the celery. Cook for 5 minutes over a moderate flame, stirring constantly. Add 1 cup of chicken stock, cover the pan and simmer for 4 minutes. Blend the sauce ingredients together and add to the pan. Continue cooking until the sauce thickens. Pour over the noodles and serve immediately.

TEA

Although Chinese wine is seldom available in the west to accompany a Chinese dinner, tea can always be had and a very good addition to the meal it is. Since the end of the war the variety of China teas available has been much smaller and quality is not all one remembers from earlier years.

To go with the meal take either green or black (which the Chinese call red) but have it in the Chinese manner, a simple infusion with no sugar or milk. There is no real substitute for English style tea at mid-afternoon but that kind of tea has no place at a Chinese dinner. Not only does China tea have good flavour but it also has a slightly astringent and cleansing quality that enables the diner to present a fresh palate to every dish that appears at the longest Chinese banquet.

Buy any good quality China tea, either the green or gunpowder type, or black of the *Kee Mun* type. Make it in the classical English way, warming the pot and then adding to the leaves fiercely boiling water. But make it weaker than for English style tea. Oddly enough, China teas are often better at the second infusion, unlike other teas which get bitter at that stage. Chinese connoisseurs of tea are known to make the first infusion, quickly pour the liquid off and concentrate on the second and better infusion.

At Chinese tables where wine isn't served the teapot is a familiar thing on the board all through the meal.

CONDIMENTS

When salt is referred to in these recipes it means ordinary
kitchen salt. This is, of course, saltier than modern table salt
which is mixed with other ingredients to keep it dry in damp
weather.

Chinese cooks use white pepper oftener than black. On the
dinner table they use a mixture of salt and pepper that is very
pleasant to the taste. The pepper ingredient is known in China
as *hua chiao*, the Latin name being Xanthoxylum. If this is
obtainable it should be heated until it is brown and crisp. It is
then rolled and pounded into a powder. Mix it in the proportion of 2 tablespoons of powdered xanthoxylum to one teaspoonful of salt. Place it in small saucers which can be bought
in any Chinese shop selling porcelain for the table. If it is not
available mix ordinary ground black pepper with salt in the
proportion of two-thirds pepper to one-third salt.

Chinese mustard is similar to English mustard and ordinary
dry mustard can be mixed with water so it is fairly liquid and
put on the table in small saucers like those used for the pepper
and salt mixture.

The idea is that any diner for whom there are insufficient
condiments in the dish being eaten can gently dip each mouthful of food with his chopsticks on its way from the dish in the
middle of the table to his mouth.

MENUS

FOR TWO PEOPLE

1 cold hors d'oeuvre
Pork with green pepper and noodles
Spring rolls
Won Ton soup
Almond tea

1 cold hors d'oeuvre
Chicken with bamboo shoots
Fried scallops
Watercress soup
Fresh fruit

1 cold hors d'oeuvre
Walnut chicken
Lamb with asparagus
Chicken mushroom soup
Grape and orange tea

1 cold hors d'oeuvre
Pork with lily buds
Butterfly shrimp
Fried rice
Lotus seed tea

Frogs' legs sauté
Beef with vegetables
Fried rice
Lychees

Filleted fish with sweet-sour sauce
Ham with spinach
Grape and orange tea

Steamed flounder
Bean sprouts with pork
Beef with cucumber
Almond tea

Won Ton soup
Fried oysters
Pineapple chicken
Fried rice
Fresh fruit

Watercress soup
Fried scallops
Pork spare-ribs
Fried rice
Candied dates

2 cold hors d'oeuvre
Chicken in paper
Roast duck
Ham and melon soup
Almond cakes

2 cold hors d'oeuvre
Minced pigeon
Canton roast pork
Almond junket

2 cold hors d'oeuvre
Spring rolls
Steamed fish with eggs
Mushrooms and water chestnuts
Fried walnuts

2 cold hors d'oeuvre
Duck liver roll
Fried rice
Fish soup
Candied dates

1 cold hors d'oeuvre
Chicken with bamboo shoot
Beef with green peppers
Meat dumplings
Almond tea

1 cold hors d'oeuvre
Chestnut chicken
Pineapple duck
Fried squab
Steamed bread (*man t'ou*)
Orange tea

1 cold hors d'oeuvre
Won Ton soup
Braised pigeon eggs
Sweet and sour fish
Pork and ginger root
Lotus seed tea

2 cold hors d'oeuvre
Pigeon with water chestnuts
Lamb with string beans
Pork with shrimps
Almond mould

2 cold hors d'oeuvre
Chicken with peppers
Cabbage soup
Beef with onions
Yangchow noodles
Almond junket

FOR PARTIES OF SIX

2 cold hors d'oeuvre
Liver croûtons
Pineapple duck
Sweet-sour fish
Won Ton soup
Roast pork
Fried rice
Almond tea

2 cold hors d'oeuvre
Fried livers
Chicken with almonds
Fried squab
Butterfly shrimp
Sweet and sour pork
Bamboo shoots and mushrooms
Watercress soup
Fried walnuts

2 cold hors d'oeuvre
Sliced beef with vegetables
Canton lobster
Pineapple duck II
Chicken velvet
Pork spare-ribs with sweet-sour sauce
Ham and melon soup
Fried rice
Orange tea

2 cold hors d'oeuvre
Chestnut chicken
Fried shrimp croûtons
Jade belt duck
Braised pigeon eggs
Pork-filled mushrooms
Fish soup
Walnut and date tea

2 cold hors d'oeuvre
Bird's nest soup
Fried sliced chicken
Steamed flounder
Bamboo shoots sauté
Beef with onions
Spring rolls
Won Ton soup
Date cakes

2 cold hors d'oeuvre
Chicken with bamboo shoots
Sweet-sour fish
Steamed duck
Pigeon with water chestnuts
Fried rice
Pork with ginger root
Egg soup
Almond tea

H

2 cold hors d'oeuvre
Pineapple sole
Fried sliced chicken
Watercress soup
Jade belt duck
Poached pigeon eggs
Minced beef with noodles
Fried rice
Walnut tea

2 cold hors d'oeuvre
Canton egg roll
Braised pheasant
Steamed flounder
Ham and cabbage soup
Fried noodles with chicken livers
Pork stuffed lotus root
Fried wild duck
Almond cakes

2 cold hors d'oeuvre
Chicken with lily buds
Minced pigeon
Won Ton soup
Fried rice
Pineapple duck
Beef with mushrooms
Shrimp croûtons
Meat dumplings
Orange tea

2 cold hors d'oeuvre
Spring rolls
Shredded liver
Chicken velvet
Watercress soup
Ham with spinach
Pineapple sole
Beef with asparagus
Fried rice
Sweet and sour carrots
Walnut and date tea

A BANQUET MENU FOR TEN PEOPLE

4 cold hors d'oeuvre
Bird's nest soup
Chicken with almonds
Prawns with asparagus
Sweet and sour pork
Braised pigeon eggs
Peking duck
Shredded liver
Chicken mushroom soup
Mushroom sauté
Steamed bread (*man t'ou*)
Braised abalone
Eight precious pudding

INDEX

227

NOTES

NOTES